by-line

Printed in the United States of America

ISBN: 978-1-59571-368-1
Library of Congress Control Number: 2009927627

Designed and published by:
Word Association Publishers
205 Fifth Avenue
Tarentum, Pennsylvania 15084
www.wordassociation.com

Designed by: Gina Datres, Word Association Publishers

by-line

**Pittsburgh's Beloved Columnist Shares
a Lifetime of Interviews and Observations**

Barbara Cloud

For

Grace Elizabeth Marie

so that you can better know, as years pass,
the lifetime privilege and joy Nana experienced
as your daddy's mother and as a journalist

contents

when

why

INTRODUCTION

At times it takes me by surprise when people approach me haltingly and then actually apologize for "bothering" me, in order to say something about a column I have written, or to say they recognize me from my picture in the newspaper. Oh, those many head shots!

Never apologize! It is such a compliment. It has always reminded me of the privilege I had all these years as a journalist. People will read my words and sometimes—the best compliment of all—tack them on their refrigerator. Perhaps this will be a book to add to your personal library.

I retired in January 2008, after fifty-five years. I haven't taken it lightly, my writing career; first, five years at the *Uniontown Evening Standard*, then thirty-six years with the *Pittsburgh Press*, and fifteen with the *Pittsburgh Post-Gazette*. It is not what I planned when I graduated from Westminster College in New Wilmington, Pennsylvania, in 1951.

I wanted to be an actress. But a funny thing happened on my way to the Broadway stage. I became a writer—temporarily, or so I thought. I needed a job. "Don't train me," I insisted when I was hired to write a personals column for my hometown newspaper back in 1952, after several unsuccessful months in New York as a showroom model on Seventh Avenue, waiting to be "discovered."

"I'm going back to New York. I am going to be an actress." I was already overacting…pretending it was so. I was following my sister, Betty Joyce, in the newspaper business in Uniontown, Pennsylvania. She was my idol…but still, I wanted to be on Broadway, not in her shoes, even though she gave me much to look up to.

Five years later, still "between engagements" (meaning "unemployed" in the theater), I dared to head to Pittsburgh and apply for an opening at the *Pittsburgh Press*. I needed to be me, but I still needed employment. My first feature by-line article in the Uniontown paper had been about a visit to a gold mine in Canada during a 1954 vacation and it is among my many crumbling clippings. So is a picture of me with my first "celebrity" interview, actor Aldo Ray, who was in Uniontown in 1955 for the opening of his film *Battle Cry*. I was twenty-six.

I thought those two stories, and more weddings and club notices than I could count, prepared me to be Brenda Starr at a major city newspaper. My acting credentials at Westminster, my three summers at Jennerstown Mountain Playhouse, earning my Actor's Equity union card, I thought, had prepared me for Broadway…if not now, soon.

I was hired at the *Press*. The journey began. Since then, in fifty years, hundreds and hundreds of interviews and columns have been tucked away. I was permitted, almost by accident, to make writing my career.

Broadway never did see me on its stages, but I passed its glittering marquees many times as I raced to and from fashion shows in New York for thirty-three years as a fashion editor. I often paused, sighed, and then scurried on to my fashion world assignments, which, I would learn, had their own theatrics. It, too, was show business.

If I could not speak words on a stage, I could put words on paper. It was a way to reach people beyond footlights and it has fulfilled me more than I could ever have expected.

Figure a column, and usually more, weekly for fifty-two weeks for fifty years, and you get the number of by-lines accumulated. Staggering.

Only a few came out of hiding for this book, carefully chosen.

Many one-on-one interviews I didn't save and wish I had: Sophie Tucker, Telly Savalas, Katharine Cornell, designer Adolfo, Erroll Garner, Gloria Swanson, Dorothy Lamour, Julie Newmar, Ginger Rogers, Vidal Sassoon, and the artist Erte.

It was a daring move for me, moving to Pittsburgh. I had never taken a journalism course. I had no typing skills but learned on my own. The *Press* didn't know quite what to do with me when I arrived in April 1957 (wearing a hat and gloves, I might add) so I wrote obituaries, pasted up a daily Patterns feature for the women's pages, started a garden club column, and still wrote announcements for weddings and engagements.

I never did learn how to spell *phaelanopsis* (the orchid commonly found in bridal bouquets), but I was in the newspaper business for good, allowing myself to satisfy the "drama" in me by writing a theater column, *In the Wings*, for twenty-five years, and, on my own time, appearing in plays at most of Pittsburgh's theaters, including the Pittsburgh Playhouse. I still thought I might be discovered. We all have dreams. They aren't always realistic.

It's called human interest, the stories I like most. It is what fulfilled me the most. Of course, the brushes with celebrity were exciting because I grew up with the movies and the Big Band era. That made meeting Tony Bennett, Harry James, Benny Goodman, Lionel Hampton, and Carmen Cavallaro special...talking to Audrey Hepburn by phone in Switzerland; Diahann Carroll in Hollywood; even Troy Donahue, if anyone remembers him as the Brad Pitt of his day...priceless.

There was Jessica Tandy, Lana Turner, Agnes Moorehead, Robert Mitchum, Danny Murtaugh, Xavier Cugat, Gertrude Berg, Cyd Charisse. Sadly, they are gone. During my career I was once accused of writing too often of "the dead or dying" and if ever that was true, it certainly is now with this collection. I make no apologies. All are worth remembering.

Yes, my age is showing. I talked to Steelers quarterback Terry Bradshaw when he was a newlywed in 1972, and a twenty-two-year-old Jane Fonda, who was in Pittsburgh in 1960 to head the Easter Parade. Calvin Klein, Oscar de la Renta, Ralph Lauren, Michael Kors, and Marc Jacobs were the new kids on the block when I was covering the fashion world, and Norman Norell, Pauline Trigère, Geoffrey Beene, Anne Klein, and Bill Blass were their peers. Now, of course, they are the veterans and, sadly, the peers are gone. Time marches on. I was privileged to see the changing of the guard, including Rudi Gernreich's topless bathing suit.

And as anyone who has followed me the past thirty-eight years knows, my son, Drew, who gives meaning to my life, grew up in the columns as I shared his childhood, and my being a single parent—rare in the '70s; his growing pains, and mine; his "adopted" aunts, Sylvia Sachs, Seima Horvitz, and Blanche Banov; his second mother/babysitter/friend Nancy French, without whom I could not have made it; and most recently, his marriage to Margaret Marie Garcia in 2007 and the arrival of my first grandchild, Grace Elizabeth Marie Cloud, on April 30, 2008.

It has even surprised me, this journey I have been privileged to take as a newspaper woman. Taking readers with me has been my greatest joy.

So, a book at last. Didn't former First Lady Barbara Bush's dog Millie write a book? Doesn't everybody write a book? Will anybody read mine? When actor Van Johnson, my teen heartthrob, died at age ninety-two last year, I was reminded: the time is now. Time waits for no one.

The stories I mention, at least some of them, needed a home. The chapters were inspired by the journalistic mantra in getting a story: WHO: people I met; WHAT: "things" which caught my eye;

WHERE: places my career took me; WHEN: nod to the past; WHY: to keep the memories alive.

I knew Bill Blass? I went to fashion shows at Pitti Palace in Florence, Italy, and the White House? I was at a Faberge party with Cary Grant? I could call Ralph Lauren on the phone and he would take my call? All that glamour? Well, yes. But there was much more as I hope this group of essays will reveal.

This isn't the story of my life. But it is the story, by example, of where my life as a journalist has taken me. It's not a tell-all book. I could never tell it all. These stories are mere samplings of where an unplanned career as a journalist took me. The biggest challenge has been the selection of material. I am grateful for all the people who have allowed me to interview them through the years, famous and not so famous. Strangers send me greeting cards and notes. I am grateful to the newspapers for which I have worked, and the people who worked beside me.

As I head toward my eightieth birthday, I feel a need to leave some footprints. As for all those people who "bother" me by saying hello on the street, on a bus, at the supermarket, at Barneys in New York City, or while walking on a beach in Stone Harbor, New Jersey, bless you. From greasepaint to printer's ink was a good move.

Besides, when I met the late actress Mady Christians, who came to lecture at Westminster College when I was an eighteen-year-old student majoring in speech and drama, she looked me up and down and told me in no uncertain terms I was not destined to be a leading lady. "You are too tall! All leading men are short." Nobody at the newspapers cared a hoot about my five-feet-ten-inch height. It was all about deadlines.

I found the role of a lifetime. I found my stage.

"I spent most of my childhood going to dancing school. I appreciate it now, but I had to miss all the parties and things kids like. I wouldn't force my girls to do that."

—Betty Grable, 1959

"I still have much work to do. They are already saying I am a star and yet I probably won't be the actress I want to be for a number of years."

—Jane Fonda, 1960

"There are no musicians in my family. They would listen to me but never took it seriously."

—Paul Anka, 1960

"Moses was the best religious role I could ever do. Christ, in my opinion, is unplayable. Many try, but I never would."

—Charlton Heston, 1962

"I was tagged as shy when I first went into the movies. Once that starts, it is never forgotten."

—Rock Hudson, 1961

"An actor can't really behave as other people do. You give up lots of gadding about during the day so you can go to work at night. That's when the ordinary person begins to wear down."

—Jessica Tandy, 1960

walter blattne
agnes moorehead
estee lauder
myrtle brady
bill blass
naomi
cordelia so
joan crawford
ethel wa
esther williamsagnes moorehead
bill blass
van johns
joan crawford
princess grace
agnes moorehead
walter blatt
myrtle brady
cordelia sc
marie maazel
phyllis dill
cordelia sc
bill blass
dr. jack knochel
galan
marvin hamlisch

Who

SPIRITUALLY RICH

When word was out that Ethel Waters would be coming to Pittsburgh to appear in a television show, her many fans shook their heads sadly, recalling the numerous stories of her failing health, unemployment, and poverty. That's been the story about Miss Waters for some time. Life had not been good to her. It's only partially true.

"I don't own anything but I don't owe anything either," she said as she observed the view of the Golden Triangle from her room on the sixth floor of the Hilton Hotel. "I'm financially poor but spiritually rich, " she said. "Money isn't the answer. I'm happier now than I have been in my whole life."

Stories of her poverty and illness circulated following a newspaper article, which the actress says shocked and embarrassed her.

The story, however, turned out to be a blessing in disguise for this veteran actress with forty years in the theater. It attracted the attention of the producers of the popular TV show *Route 66*. They set out to find a show for her and are filming it here.

"God brought me the job," she continued, "and I have a belief. It's the Waters belief but it has brought me contentment few people know. I found that by turning to my Lord."

Miss Waters has always let it be known her belief in Christianity came before anything. "There are certain things I won't do because of my beliefs, not for any other reason. I won't sell out. This has caused me to be black-listed, red-listed, blue-listed, whatever you want to call it, even among my own people. I was offered $75,000 for my life story, with changes "here and there," but I've turned it down.

"I cry very little because I have a lot to be thankful for. The word 'star' is a high-sounding name. It's fine when you're on that stage, but after that you're a lost ball in the high weeds."

She said she used to shake hands with hundreds of people who came to see her perform, and then she would go back to her room and cry her eyes out. "I was so lonely. It's not that way now. The Lord and I have a running conversation."

She lives in Pasadena. Her home for twenty years gave way to the Los Angeles freeway. She said she didn't mind leaving. It had served its purpose, but she was glad nobody else would be living in it.

"I was very sick for a long time," she said. "My weight gave me a heart condition, although I feel better now than in ages. I've lost ninety pounds and am trying to lose fifty more."

The actress, who appeared on Broadway in *Member of the Wedding* in the 1950s, will be sixty-one on October 31 and she has a great faith reasoning why things happen. "Whatever I do I do with all of me," she said, "and that includes my faith."

She hugged me as I left our interview. "God bless you," she whispered in my ear. I somehow felt sure her wish went straight to God's ear. I feel better having met her.

CLANG, CLANG, CLANG ...

September 1964

You don't meet people much nicer than Ralph Johnson. In a world filled with mud-slinging politicians, racial antagonists, and unrest in Vietnam, it is nice to be able to say you know someone like him.

Ralph is a streetcar conductor. As I reflect, I don't really know much about him at all, except what I see briefly pretty much on a daily basis as I make my way to work. He likes to go fishing, he spends many of his summer vacations in Canada, his son plays football, and he lives in Glassport, Pennsylvania. That much I know.

He is one of the friendliest conductors guiding those long cars along the Fifth Avenue East End route and he has a greeting for practically all of his regular riders. He knows most of them by name.

When you are a bit grumpy in the morning and have skipped breakfast, gotten a run in your stocking, managed to guide a skirt zipper off its track at the last minute but have to get to the streetcar stop by 8:32 a.m., the day looks rotten at best.

But there's Ralph, pulling that signal cord on the trolley as a wake-up welcome and then a cheerful, "Hi, Barb, where ya been the last couple of days?"

It's refreshing. And sadly I think it is the exception rather than the rule. Here is a man who seems to love his job and love people. Would that there were more like him.

Ralph remembers little things about his regulars. He'll talk to you about your sick sister, your dog, the score of the game between your high school or college football teams. How does he do that, day after day?

The policewomen and crossing guards at various corners

wave good morning. He'll open his door at the stoplight and talk to Mary about her boyfriend and more than once he has stopped the trolley and left his seat to help an older woman laden with bundles scramble up the steps on a rainy day.

Here is a man who is a pleasant surprise to all who plunk their thirty cents into the coin box, prepared to be glum as a new day begins. He'll have them smiling before the next block, and he'll do it every day. That's worth a lot more than thirty cents.

IT'S A JUNGLE

May 1965

There was the quiet buzz of young girls' whispers in the Chatham College classroom. Then Mildred Evanson, who teaches in the speech and drama department, hurried to the front of the room and happily announced, "She's coming!"

There was a hushed silence as the door opened. Agnes Moorehead, an accomplished actress on both stage and screen, had spent a few days on the campus and all the students enjoyed meeting and talking with her. Here was a woman who knew first-hand what it was like to be part of the theater world. And although all of the girls aren't planning to be actresses, many hope to work in the theater in some way.

They stared at Miss Moorehead, as did I, in awe. They listened attentively as that familiar voice recalled experiences as the only female member of the touring company of George Bernard Shaw's *Don Juan in Hell* with Cedric Hardwicke, Charles Laughton, and Charles Boyer. Her name-dropping, done without affectation, left their eyes shining with contemplation about the associations they also might have one day.

When she talked about Orson, it was Mr. Welles, of course. Charles, naturally, was Mr. Laughton. "Touring with such a show," she said, "was like having a finishing course in Shaw."

The students laughed when Miss Moorehead frowned at the idea of having my photographer take candids of her as she talked, explaining "After doing Velma (an unkempt hag in the film *Hush, Hush Sweet Charlotte*) I know I shouldn't worry, but I don't want to look like a witch all of the time. I tend to get my face all screwed up when I talk."

She did just that, and often. It's part of what makes Agnes Moorehead the legend she is. Then, back to *Don Juan*.

"If I never acted again, I would be happy having done this show," she said. When she described Laughton as a man with a heart like "pink plush," their faces lit up. Hardwicke, she said, who sat behind her in the reading, would tease her after each show with, "You've got one more freckle on your back."

And then the room was quiet as she sighed and softly said, "It is too bad Charles and Cedric are gone. They brought us great entertainment."

Miss Moorehead talked about Emlyn Williams, and Marcel Marceau with whom she studied mime. She talked about the value of pauses in delivery of long speeches, change of tempo and pitch, and breaking down thoughts, and also of friends who opened doors for her. "I know what works. I know what has worked for me. The magic of acting is being able to get over that imaginary wall, the empathy of the actor to the audience, and back again. No one can explain it."

When two of the students did scenes from Shakespeare, the actress observed them pensively. One of the students said she was having trouble relaxing. "We all have trouble relaxing," was Miss Moorehead's answer. "John Gielgud said it took him twenty years to relax. But you must learn to make nervousness work for you."

When it was time for the class to end, she made her most pointed remark. "It's a jungle, believe me. I don't care who the actor is, he worries every day about his next role, hoping it will be as good or better than the last. The best advice I can give to the aspiring actress going into this jungle is to be sincere, polite, and willing to work and to learn. But I know some girls just won't take it."

And then the spell was broken. A lesson in acting, but maybe even more had been learned. I couldn't take my eyes off her hands and arm gestures. They spoke volumes.

MODEL OF SUCCESS

August 1969

She's just twenty-one and she has the world on a string. That string is attached to a photo lens. She's Naomi Sims and she is one of the top models in the country.

She also happens to call Pittsburgh her home although her residence is Gramercy Park in New York. From this site she packs her luggage and travels to such glamorous places as Argentina, Brazil, Hawaii, Rome, Barcelona, and Bermuda.

"I am deliriously happy," says Naomi following a photo assignment to Greece for *Time* magazine. "I love to travel and I particularly like to visit and live with people in their homes in the various countries. I have made some marvelous friends. When I can divorce myself from New York, I am happy," she sighed. "It is hectic living in New York."

As hectic as it might be, Naomi has conquered one of the most difficult cities in the world and one of the most competitive careers. Now, wherever she goes, she is recognized. In a city where recognition doesn't come easily, this is quite an accomplishment. And Naomi is impressed. "To be recognized and stopped on the street? It is just marvelous," she said.

"You know, Greece was very cold. If you saw the layout of pictures from that trip, you might remember the photograph of me wearing the metal breastplate, a new fashion idea. You can imagine how it felt with that cold steel in that cold weather, and we were supposed to look warm."

That was just one of the little inconveniences Naomi must put up with as a model. But at $60 an hour, wouldn't you?

Naomi attended Westinghouse High School. She was always

self-conscious about her height.

Can you imagine! I was five feet one in 1959 and by the time I was fourteen, I had reached my present height, which is five feet ten. I guess I always wanted to be a model. But my parents didn't understand that it could be a career and pay well. They wanted me to go to school. I knew that I wanted to be involved in fashion in some way. I went to the Fashion Institute in New York and took some university courses at night."

Naomi went to New York in June of 1967. By August she had decided to give the modeling world a whirl.

"A friend gave me the name of a photographer," she said. The photographer just happened to be Goasta Peterson, whose wife, Patricia, writes fashion for the *New York Times*.

Naomi's very first assignment had her appearing on the cover of a *New York Times* magazine fashion supplement. The rest reads like a fairy tale. Naomi has been in constant demand ever since.

As an African American, Naomi has broken many barriers. She was the first black model to appear in a television commercial and the first to appear on the cover of a major magazine, *Ladies Home Journal*. She's also the first black model to get a multicolor magazine spread (*Vogue*) and the first to pose for national ads alone and not among a crowd of white models.

"I used to be an emaciated 120 pounds and even went as low as 116," she said. "I really dieted. Then when I went to Europe, I ate all that marvelous food and put the weight on again. I came back to New York and the pace made me lose it again."

But after another trip out of the country "where everything is relaxed," Naomi gained weight and is now 135 pounds. "It is much better and I look healthy. The photographers agree," she said.

Her daily menu usually includes a breakfast of soft-boiled egg, raisin toast, and coffee with ice cream in it. "At lunch I am usually rushed so I have a hamburger or something. And at night I eat out a lot. I'm single, you know, although I am seeing someone regularly, and we often dine out. I like to cook and although my mother never really taught me, I invent things. I never just have a can of soup but I add something to it."

Cosmetics, she said, were a problem at first. "There are many colors and skin types for the black woman," she explained. "First of all, I am against powder for dark skin. I use moisturizers. I like reds and yellows and I like the skin to shine. I do my own makeup and I experiment. I'm always changing. I like a dark purple eye shadow with a lid gloss over it for my eyes and I wear thick false lashes on top and bottom."

She prefers simple, elegant clothes in her personal wardrobe and wears pants with skinny tops during the day. "Great for climbing in and out of taxis," she said. "Everyone in New York is wearing pants. In Europe in the most sophisticated places, even in Spain, women are wearing pants."

So Naomi prefers to go the opposite in the evening. She wears short dresses to show off her very long legs. She also likes colorful hairnets or snoods and maybe a flower in her hair. She prefers white or black for dramatic clothes.

"The life of a model is short lived," said Naomi thoughtfully. "I'm enjoying it while I can and keeping as busy as I can. I can't believe all of this has happened to me. I'm thinking it might be fun to try acting, too, but right now I'm too busy."

THIS VAN'S ON THE MOVE

October 1976

In 1945 there was a new Hollywood find. He was freckled and snub-nosed and he became the bobbysoxers' idol. I was one of those bobbysoxers. At that time, I was sure I was the only one…that Van Johnson and I were going to meet, fall in love, and get married. Such is the way of youth, crushes, and movie mania.

Who would have thought, thirty-one years later, I would be chatting with him as casually as if he were my neighbor. He's just about to tackle the lead role in *Music Man* in San Jose, California.

"I played the role in London for a year and a half," he said, "but can you imagine my nerve doing it now at age sixty?"

The London engagement was about fifteen years ago, although he did do the exhausting role of Professor Harold Hill in a straw-hat production three summers ago. "Of course, I might be in better shape now," he said. "I've stopped smoking—through hypnotism. Now if someone could just hypnotize me to stop eating…"

Johnson's days at Metro-Goldwyn-Mayer were very much as reported by other stars of those days. "We were family. Mr. Mayer took very good care of us," said Johnson, who was with the studio for twenty years.

"I still keep in touch with many of them, particularly the girls. June Allyson just called, as a matter of fact, to invite me to her wedding, but I won't be able to make it. As family, we all worried about each other, grieved for each other. But there's no nostalgia on my part. I don't think that much about the past."

Johnson said he came out of his long film career in good shape financially, due to the wise judgment of his business manager and a good pension fund. "I'm a Virgo, and Swedish, too," he said, chuckling that very familiar way which won him the hearts of young girls like myself in the '40s.

"Actually, I'm a recluse. I have two cats, I read, do needlepoint, and paint. I live in a penthouse in New York, right next to Greta Garbo." That, in itself, must be exciting for Johnson. The great Garbo was one of his idols when he was a young lad sitting in movie audiences. "She still has that magnificent face," he said.

The needlepoint, he explained, came about when he had surgery for cancer a few years ago. "I needed something to keep my mind occupied and one of the nurses showed me how it was done," he said. "I was hooked, if you'll pardon the pun. I've done about eighty-five pillows and the dining room chairs, all in one stitch."

Johnson and I chatted by phone while he was appearing in Oklahoma City in *Send Me No Flowers*. He says it is one of his favorite plays.

"I'm a positive thinker," he said, regarding his bout with cancer. "I carry God in my heart and so far, I seem to be doing just fine. I'm one of the lucky ones. I can do just about anything, but I really couldn't take a TV series. But I would like to do a Broadway musical. That way I could settle down in New York. I always seem to be packing to go. TWA is home," he laughed.

"I love New York. I lived in California, of course, but I decided the sun had been beating on this red hair too long. I had started out in New York, pounding pavements for seven years before movies came along. Stage is my first love." It was in *Pal Joey* on Broadway that he and Gene Kelly caught the eyes of film producers and were whisked to the West Coast.

Johnson admits he used to be a movie fan, but he never goes now. "I'm square," he admitted. "I don't understand porno and all the four-letter words."

Married once, now divorced from Evie Wynn, he has a twenty-six-year-old daughter, Schuyler. He says he will never marry again.

DEMANDS ARE DECEIVING

May 1977

Some people leave impressions, indelibly etched. Joan Crawford, who died recently, was such a person. We met several times.

The things I remember most were her carrot-red hair, her diminutive size, her attitude of total control at one meeting and her pathetic, insecure, and agitated mood a few years later.

Being of an age which most definitely includes years of Saturday afternoon matinees beginning at eleven cents a throw, I was awe-struck by the likes of Crawford, and an early assignment to interview her was close to traumatic.

The actress was in Pittsburgh in 1958 with her husband, Alfred Steele, chairman of the board of the Pepsi Cola Company. It was his image she wanted to project during that visit, but it was obvious all the media gathered in the William Penn Hotel suite couldn't have cared less about Steele.

Each time she was approached by a reporter, she turned the conversation toward the man whose arm she clung to...her husband. It was very womanly, and just what you might expect from one of her movies. Nobody really cared about the new soft drink plant, but in each photo, she insisted the product be in full view.

She was in command...no doubt about that. There are probably some old-timers on the hotel staff who remember well the list which preceded her scheduled visit to any city.

Although the total list can't be recalled, I do know she insisted on certain types of flowers for her room, an adjacent room for her maid, a refrigerator stocked with Pepsi, a certain brand of candy on the coffee table...the list was lengthy and somewhat eccentric in demands, but worthy of a product of the Hollywood star system, it seemed.

I recall she delighted in telling everyone she fixed her husband's breakfast every morning. And when I blurted out the fact that she wasn't as tall as I had imagined from all her films, she looked at me and raised that famous heavy eyebrow, pulled back the familiar heavily padded shoulders, and declared "I walk tall (and then the proper Crawford pause for dramatic effect)…and I think tall."

Steele died not too long after that visit. Our next meeting was in 1968, when she came to Pittsburgh to do commentary for a millinery show at Kaufmann's Department Store.

She sat in her hotel suite with her feet tucked under her, looking like a small sparrow, her eyes the biggest part of her. She had kicked off her shoes and appeared smaller than her five feet four inches. She paced the room nervously, calling the switchboard repeatedly to inquire about some fans for her room. Her hair was unkempt, her speech hesitant and low key, except for the anxiety. Her dress, hat, and gloves were all in a matching color and she chattered nervously with the store fashion assistant concerning the speech she wanted to give to the women who had come to see her.

In spite of time, the crowds were four deep. They didn't seem to mind that she kept them waiting for at least forty-five minutes as she primped in front of a mirror and demanded just one more run-through of her remarks.

Eventually, she felt she had pulled herself together. I will never forget her as she walked from the room. She turned to me, her eyes almost pleading, and said ever so quietly, "Do I look all right?"

A piece of cotton was stuck to the heavy beaded necklace she wore. I reached over and removed it. "Just fine," I said.

BUSTLIN' AT 96

April 1978

There is so much beauty in Myrtle Brady, it should be caught in the wind and scattered wherever there is blight—wherever despair dwells, wherever misery, loneliness, and self-pity have taken root. The likes of this tiny woman are seldom seen today.

She was ninety-six on Thursday. But as warm as her gaze can be, as gentle as the touch of her arthritic fingers are to your arm, don't take her for a softie.

She's up at 5:00 a.m. every day. She has no time to be lonely because she's too busy chopping wood for her stove, cutting back the grape vines, cooking three square meals for herself and any neighbor in Ross Township she invites to share her table, making pounds of soap, planting and weeding her garden. She eats from her garden for three months and from her cellar (she cans everything) the other nine.

"They humor old people too much today," said Mrs. Brady. "If they'd do more, they'd be better off. Maybe people won't like that I said that, but I believe it."

While she talked, Mrs. Brady had the whole stovetop going, as well as the oven, on her stove, a Kalamazoo, which must be fifty years old. It's easily her favorite item in the entire house, which she and her late husband built and lived in most of their married life. He passed away twenty years ago.

"If I had to give up my wood stove, it would be like part of me," she said, opening the bottom door to check on a pan of home-baked rolls.

On the cabinet counter was a just-baked apple pie. In the saucepans, corn, green beans, mashed potatoes, and chicken gravy. There was also a dish of cucumber pickles and another of large red beets. "This is all from my garden, except for the chickens," she said, chuckling. "I used to have my own chickens for eggs, but it got to be too much."

Neighbors, who have been gathering to help Mrs. Brady observe her birthdays for at least fifteen years, testify to her incredible energy as well as her loving spirit and bright sense of humor.

Is she happiest when she is tending her garden? She thought for a moment. "I'm happy no matter what I am doing," she said. "I am never despondent, never. I guess I got close to being depressed this past winter because of the cold and not being able to get out. But I was born and raised on a farm in Ohio. I'm used to hard work. I milked cows, slopped hogs, fed the chickens, and watered the horses.

"I was twenty-nine when I married my husband. We built two rooms and lived out of them and then added on as years went on. I used to drive a Model-T and I miss the long walks my husband and I used to take. We had two acres of land here and I guess we'd walk over a couple of miles every day."

Many, many years ago, when people were dropping like flies, she had the flu and typhoid fever. She lost most of her hair and the doctor gave her little chance of recovery.

"We moved here to fresh air and I knew I'd never move back to the city," she said. "I think that's what saved me. I don't think I spent $50 on doctors. I take no medicine and I eat ham and eggs and grapefruit every morning."

She fell a few weeks ago and might have cracked a rib or two, but she simply taped them and went out and raked some leaves.

"All I do is cook, it seems," she said, adding quickly, "but I love it. I eat lots of rhubarb…it's starting to come up in the garden now…and I love dandelion greens. I guess that's where I get my medicine."

Mrs. Brady makes her own lard, her own bread, her own sauerkraut.

She just finished making 116 pounds of soap, which she swears clears up skin problems. She has a paperboy, she says, who will be eternally grateful to her for giving him a bar. "He was around the other day to remind me he was just about out of soap," she said with a grin. "I told him it got rid of wrinkles too…just look at me."

Young people love her. She loves being with them.

She blames television for much of the violence in the world today and the unrest among young people. She only likes to watch ball games and, before that, wrestling.

"I think I'm ninety-six because of the way I eat," she said, suddenly turning serious. "The only thing I eat out of a can is pineapple. I've never had a store-bought pie in my life."

Now that the days are warming, she's anxious to get to her garden. Close at her heels is her dog, Cindy, and somewhere on the property are five cats.

This past winter, she admits, her house got a bit cold. Relatives wanted her to come and stay with them, but Mrs. Brady said there would be nobody to take care of her dog and cats. "They were cold too," she said. "I wouldn't leave them."

Mrs. Brady sat in her rocker and Cindy was on her lap in a flash. "She's a good dog, not worth a darn," said her mistress, fondly stroking the black and white fur.

Mrs. Brady doesn't have time to sulk or let things get her down.

She has a theory. "If you're too lazy to cook," she says, "you shouldn't be allowed to eat."

And with that, she started doing her dishes. Guests aren't permitted to help. It's one thing that makes her frown.

DOLLARS AND SCENTS

You hear the name. You see the name. You wear, yes, even smell like the name. Estee Lauder.

Who is she? What is she like? Does she ever move outside her incredibly beautiful offices in the General Motors Building in New York? Is there more to her life than being seen at all the best parties in all the best places, wearing all the best clothes?

The corporate color is blue. Nobody has to tell you that. Even if you were not aware of all the packaging on Lauder products, you would know it as soon as you step off the elevator, your ears cracking from the rapid ascent to the 37th-floor majestic empire this tiny woman has amassed.

Pre-warned, you might say, honey-haired Mrs. Lauder likes to do instant make-overs when she spots a woman who needs a beauty product or two to improve her face. I felt as if I was certainly going to be told my skin was too dry, and that I should stay out of the strong sun. For starters, that is.

And I was. As soon as Mrs. Lauder meets you, she does a study of your face, and it isn't done in an unkind way. Just relentless. She simply feels so strongly about her commitment to beauty—she's not just pulling in the money and laughing about female gullability when it comes to promoting products.

"Come into the dining room," she says. In the dining room there is a display of all her products, arranged according to the years the various scents were introduced. She surveyed the table. "Just for you," she said, indicating the thought which went into the planned interview.

"Ummmm, it smells wonderful in here," I commented. Mrs.

Lauder's nose was moving in another direction. "I smell narcissus," she said, looking around for the offender.

Sure enough, there were fresh narcissus plants around the very pretty display of her latest success, White Linen. It was detracting from the scents: Azuree, Estee, Youth Dew, Cinnabar, and Aliage, and Aramis for men, which she knows as well as her own children's names. The potted narcissus plants were removed from the room.

"I love what I do. I thrive on it. I am interested in everything beautiful and that includes a party, a place, people. I don't tire of the socializing. I find that if I can go home after hours in the office and rest for just a half hour, I am then ready to go on to dinner or a party.

"I worry about my customers," she adds, signaling a secretary to get someone on the phone for her. And, just then, a call from Paris, which she must take. "Excuse me, have a cookie and some tea. I'll be right back."

During our conversation, Mrs. Lauder was to excuse herself several times in order to get something off her mind or to make contact with someone by phone.

"Now, where were we?" she said, sitting down and studying the display of her fragrances, questioning her employees when she found one or two items missing from the tray of unusual pill boxes which she has offered as gifts in various seasons.

She squinted and looked at me again. "You look so much better, you see? You didn't need much, but the blush makes a difference. My family were all skin doctors," she adds, sipping her tea. "I wanted to be a doctor, and I guess that is why I feel so strongly about treatment products as well as the cosmetics.

"I now wear White Linen all the time," she says. "The name seems to declare something clean and crisp, and that's what it is.

Do you know there are twenty-eight ingredients in White Linen? I think you need a different scent for summer, just like you change from a fur coat to a lighter weight."

Of all cosmetics, she says she never believed in false eyelashes. "I never liked the idea of eyes preceding women into the room," she said, leaning in to her secretary, who had again excused herself for interrupting the conversation.

"The woman from the *London Times* is here," she said.

"Come into my office," she motioned to me. "It's getting too noisy in here. She sat down behind her antique table desk. On one table, in sterling silver or antique frames, photographs of chums— the Duchess of Windsor, Cardinal Terrence Cook, and Princess Caroline of Monaco. From a window, a magnificent view of Central Park.

"Makeup in the '80s must look good and do good. Someone's name on a label isn't going to impress the public the way it does now," says Mrs. Lauder. "Products will have to perform."

FASHIONABLE FRIENDS

November 1982

Vera Maxwell, who has been designing clothes the major portion of her eighty years, was seated behind her desk in her small office on New York's Seventh Avenue.

She looked up as I entered and she pushed aside the long yellow legal pad on which she was writing.

She looked thinner than I remembered, but she was smiling and her white hair was pulled back with a ribbon. She was dressed in black, which somehow seemed significant.

The designer was a close friend of the late Princess Grace of Monaco. Close might not accurately cover their friendship of many years. It was much more like mother and daughter.

Her openness and her willingness to reminisce about her friendship with the princess, who died September 14 as the result of injuries from an auto accident in Monaco, is helping her accept the tragedy.

She pointed to the paper on her desk. "Funny, but I was just finding a moment to write to Rainier," she said, allowing me to look at her bold script on the note pad. "I was telling him I hoped the short rest in Nassau with the children would ease the ache and the loneliness."

She says she is still not over the shock. "I can't believe I won't look up and see that beautiful girl," she said, glancing at a photo of the royal family, which was just above sketches of her own grandchildren.

She had been at the Monaco palace, an annual trip, just three weeks before the accident. She flew back immediately when she learned the princess had died. Ironically, she said, she had made a black coat for Prince Rainier that very week and was about to send it to him.

"But never for anything like this," she said sadly. "He likes comfortable clothes and I have made several jackets for him. I thought how nice this black coat would look with white slacks. I was thinking of it for happy times."

Miss Maxwell looks much younger than her eighty years and has been designing clothes since 1947. The designer is an elegant but comfortable-to-be-with woman. In 1966, when I first interviewed her, there was a transit strike in New York and in extremely cold weather she had walked forty blocks from her office for our interview. Her cook had failed to show up and she prepared an evening snack for us.

And while she bustled about, I wandered through her apartment, noticing particularly the amazing number of photographs of Princess Grace and her family on shelves and tables. Some were informal snapshots Miss Maxwell had taken herself.

"We became friends when we were both cited for fashion awards in 1955 at Neiman Marcus," she had explained in the earlier interview. "Grace is a lovely girl. She's one woman who always manages to look right. She really enjoyed the poetry (readings) as much as anything she had done in past years," said Miss Maxwell, who traveled to Pittsburgh to hear her friend two years ago when she was a guest of the International Poetry Forum.

"In spite of what you hear, she was very happy with her life. She loved her husband and her children and Monaco. She had problems with her children at times. Who hasn't? But their father says they have been wonderful through all of this, particularly Caroline."

WALTER ON WALNUT

June 1984

Almost any day of the week, except for the European vacations or trips to the New York fashion market, Walter Blattner is a familiar figure on Walnut Street in Shadyside. He owns a lot of it, for one thing.

Many people stroll through their garden and proudly recall when they planted that first shrub, the towering birch, or the row of peonies.

Blattner can stand at either end of Walnut Street and do the same. The garden has surely grown. He planted one of the first seeds in 1955 when he opened the boutique Surrey on what was then a very dreary street.

Always conservatively dapper, he surveys the goings-on, the people. He likes watching people.

He admits that today's Surrey, housed in Bellefonte Place, is aimed at the young, well-to-do customer, usually one who is preppy or trendy.

He's not looking to offer bargains, or to please all the people. He knows who his customer is. She has some cash to spend. She'll spend it easily for something special.

Blattner, 63, had major surgery several weeks ago at Shadyside Hospital. It turned out well and he feels very, very fortunate. He's sniffing the air and smelling the flowers with a new zest. That's all he will say. As visual as he is, he is reluctant to talk about his personal life.

Blattner was with Kaufmann's at one time and has been retailing for forty years. He's a character, a man of moods—confident, sometimes curt, thoughtful, and enigmatic to many. You can walk into his store and hardly notice he is standing back in a corner—

observing, thinking, smiling.

He has never sought publicity. But he likes to reminisce. With his slightly clipped German accent (he came to the United States from Germany when he was fifteen), he can sit in his office above the store for hours on end.

He opened his first Surrey in 1953 in the Union Trust Building on Grant Street, Downtown. At the time it was the talk of the town because of its avant-garde approach. Next came the first Shadyside store in 1955.

In 1964, he moved the Grant Street Surrey to what he thought would be fashionable Oliver Avenue. It was at the corner of Oliver and Liberty Avenues. But stores began to vacate in 1967 to make way for Oliver Tyrone Corporation's buildings and plaza. By 1968, Oliver Avenue had all but disappeared.

The Downtown store was in addition to the Shadyside spot, but certainly more posh. Even when he moved to the Oliver-Liberty spot, Blattner kept a shop at his original Grant Street site. But clearly, the Downtown store was an expansion of all that Blattner believed in. And it was elegant. Louis Talotta and George R. Simons created the atmosphere as decorator and architect. The most spectacular additions were the eighteen-foot gates at the entrance, antiqued and made to look old. They even had an antique padlock, once part of a Spanish jail.

Blattner smiles when he remembers that venture. "I've always wanted a trademark," he had exclaimed at the time the new store was adding excitement to Pittsburgh's first Renaissance. "I think I've found it with these gates."

Nothing pleased Blattner more than showing off the newest fashions from Europe. "Here's what they are wearing in Paris," he would say of items he had brought back from his overseas buying trips. Labels in his store inventory were just as likely to be from

Spain, Paris, Rome, or London, as New York. Now, foreign labels are common, but in 1964 it was daring and different.

The move to Shadyside in 1955, however, was a gamble. Walnut Street was not exactly chic at the time, but several familiar nightspots were quite popular. A young crowd was already familiar with Fox's, The Casbah, and Hollywood Social Club, and the Shadyside Theater, which played art films. The Shadyside Surrey became successful and was the catalyst for the many shops that were to follow.

Blattner moved Surrey from one side of Walnut to the nearby Aiken Avenue village shops in 1958. He and two partners built the Aiken complex. Then he took over the corner of Walnut and Bellefonte in 1970, and Surrey had yet another new home.

The entire corner was reconstructed in 1982 and became Bellefonte Place, which Blattner owns. He also owns The Theatre Complex, site of the old Shadyside movie house. In 1976, he opened still another store there called Topaz, to carry designer lines. It lasted two years.

You can't argue with his success. But Blattner sounds almost sad when he discusses the reason he finds himself in the business of retailing and developing.

"I had no talent. I couldn't play the piano. I tried. I couldn't paint. I tried that, too," he explained while lunching on cold salad at Le Petit Café, right next to his store. "So, since I couldn't be an artist or a musician, I have tried to use development as a means of expression.

"You have to feel it here," he said, pointing to his stomach, "whether it is right or not. You sense trends. What will be good, and then, when to get rid of it. You either have that gut feeling or you don't."

MAMA OF A SPORT

March 1989

It was like going back in time—to movie theaters on Saturday afternoons. Here I was, talking to Esther Williams. I felt like a chlorine groupie.

"Miss Williams, I saw all your pictures…several times. I tried to swim like you. I tried smiling underwater but always got a mouthful. I wanted my hair to look as smooth and shiny as yours. For ten years I did the backstroke in my sleep."

And I did. So did lots of others.

"You know why you like to remember?" she asked. "It recalls a happier time. Those years really were happier times."

This is a candid mermaid who admits to turning sixty-five last August. In 1963, she married one of her leading men, Fernando Lamas, and chose to fade into the background as a wife and mother. She had three children by a previous marriage, and Lamas, who died in 1982, had a young son, Lorenzo. He wanted his wife to be a homebody. She didn't mind.

Now she's taking another plunge, moving from MGM studio dressing rooms to dressing rooms in stores all across the country. She is designing—or helping to design—swimsuits for Misty Swimwear.

She started competitive swimming as a California teenager and was considered a certain candidate for the 1940 Olympics. But World War II changed all that. She joined the Billy Rose Aquacade, where she was spotted by MGM. She went on to make twenty-six movies, capitalizing on her swimming ability and good looks. When she started, she made $75 a week, and after fourteen years, she was still making just $200.

Who better to dress women for splish-splashing? She designed many of the suits she wore in her films. She is considered the creator of the backyard pool, with six hundred companies carrying the Esther Williams brand. She's also into spas.

She was interviewed for this story by phone from Beverly Hills, where she just had her morning swim with Max, her schnauzer. He was a gift from her stepson, Lorenzo. Her other children, Benjamin, Kimball, and Susie, are from her marriage to Ben Gage, and she is a grandmother.

"I refuse to deprive myself of eating the things I like," she admitted. "I want to feel fit. I don't worry about the extra weight. I'm sure there are lots of women like me. We don't look like the *Sports Illustrated* models."

She became aware of her contribution to synchronized swimming when she was asked to do color commentary at the Olympic Games in 1984 in Los Angeles.

"It's great being the mama of a sport. The coaches and the parents and grandparents of the swimmers in those games were in the movie audiences in the '40s when we did the swim musicals. I saw how water ballet had mushroomed. I felt honored."

She laughs about some of her movie swimsuits. One was encrusted with mirrors and another was a heavy wool plaid. Both caused her to sink when she dove into the water. That's when they started listening to her suggestions about design.

COURAGE OF A COUTURIER

March 1991

Nobody calls him James or Jim. He's known as Jimmy. Or Mr. Galanos. Or simply, Galanos.

He is considered the lone survivor of a dying art in America. It's called couture. Although he makes clothes that are sold "off the rack" in upscale stores, he is considered the equal of the great couturiers of Paris. American designers Norman Norell, Adrian, Mainbocher, Charles James, and Hattie Carnegie once occupied the same lofty perch, but now they're all gone. Galanos's clothes are as finely tailored as their French counterparts, with insides as luxurious as the outsides.

The Galanos label also commands the highest prices in the country, although fashions from Bill Blass, Bob Mackie, and Geoffrey Beene come close. New York publicist Eleanor Lambert calls Galanos the "guru on the mountainside" and the "saving grace of American haute couture."

"Custom dressmaking is almost dead," she explains. "He has remained successful because he has always been a tidy, self-contained entity—a one-man band."

He also chooses to show his collection in a New York hotel suite, not in a glitzy runway presentation. And he does it months later than other major American designers and a few weeks after the French collections. In mid-February, he spent two weeks with store buyers in New York. He designs the clothes. He sells the clothes, too.

Galanos stands alone, a singular sign of an art form that is fast disappearing. Indeed, it might be gone except for his determination to make aesthetically handsome clothes in an age when the lowest price, not aesthetics, guides most customers into the stores.

Galanos himself doesn't deny he is a loner personally as well as professionally. "I love people but I know how to be alone," says the sixty-six-year-old designer, who became prominent during the Reagan administration. Nancy Reagan wore his gowns at the inauguration balls in 1981 and 1985.

The son of Greek immigrants, Galanos was born in Philadelphia. He attended Traphagen School of Fashion in New York City for just eight months in 1940 and had trouble breaking into the city's Seventh Avenue garment center. He does, however, recall seeing one of his designs earn half a million dollars for the manufacturer. Galanos had sold it for five dollars. He never looked back. He has remained in California because he likes the climate. Or maybe because that's where he had his first real taste of success.

Consider that he has his workrooms and factory on what he terms "the wrong side of the tracks" in Los Angeles. From downtown Los Angeles it is a twenty-five-dollar cab ride to South Sepulveda Boulevard in West Los Angeles. It is not Beverly Hills. The small factory was once an RCA technical lab. He bought it thirty years ago. The entrance is right off the sidewalk. There's no lyrical winding drive to an estate, no atelier with plush carpet and crystal chandeliers. It is so lacking in pomp, you check the street address again. The name plate was on the white brick wall of a building that could be a low-rise neighborhood garage.

"I don't need a fancy office to inspire me," says the man whose "little nothing" dresses start at $4,900. His small office, so conspicuously neat, has stacks of magazines piled to the ceiling, all perfectly in line, arranged behind his desk.

Soft-spoken and gracious, Galanos is a surprise. Early pictures of him reveal a kind of flamboyant style—a pinstriped suit and a polka-dot shirt and tie. I expected him to be intimidating, immodest, and impatient and bored with the interview.

Deciding what I should wear for this interview took more time than usual. I felt sure he would notice. After all, he had once remarked after observing some fashion professionals, "God, *these* are the arbiters of fashion?"

He also believes fashion magazines and the new school of fashion photographers are the worst offenders in propagating terrible taste. "There's no such thing as taking a picture of somebody who looks like a lady. Models today are always turned into sex symbols."

So when he complimented me on what I was wearing—white pants, brown jacket, and gold silk blouse—I warmed to him immediately. My outfit was not couture, not even close. But he was a gentleman. One glance at his neatly arranged office clutter and you knew he appreciated cleanliness as well as style. I knew I had cleanliness. And I was not a sex symbol. I was in.

As it turned out, Galanos was anxious to finish the interview, but not because he was too important for it. His mind, obviously, was on the workroom just a few feet away. He was anxious to get back because he was putting together his spring collection.

He has a devoted staff from all over the world. He calls them his League of Nations. "They never take shortcuts," he once told a reporter for *Connoisseur* magazine.

And there he was among them at 9:00 a.m., talking to one of his seventy-five employees. A piece of magnificent gold lace was spread out on the table in front of him, ready to be cut. He had been there since eight o'oclock.

With fabrics at $350 a yard, you think long and hard before you cut. Among his employees are patternmakers, cutters, pressers, and tailors. The bulk of them work on construction and hand details.

In a throw-away age he still believes in quality workmanship, hand-finishing, and tailoring. And there is always the client who is willing to pay for it, although even Galanos wonders what the future holds.

Galanos smiles when he recalls the impact he and Rudi Gernreich had as California designers daring to invade New York in the early '60s. He remembers people asking, "Who are these kids?"

"A paper cup is as elegant as I get in my office," he said, explaining the cups for our coffee. "I work with my people. I don't usually dress like this. I put on a tie just for you."

He was relaxed, pleasant, nice. He excused himself only once to settle a matter in the workroom. On his green marble desk, in perfect order just like his magazines, was an almost empty jar of jelly beans, a gift from President Reagan.

Galanos smiled. "That's the original engraved jar he sent when he was elected but as you can see, he didn't ever refill it."

He misses the days of the glamorous stars. He wanted to go into films when he first started designing, and for a time worked as a sketch artist for Jean Louis, head designer at Columbia Studios. He also did wardrobes for Rosalind Russell and later for a play on Broadway before going into business.

"There's no glamour image today. It is nonexistent. I go to the movies today to see a wonderful performance, but I don't know the new stars. I hate the way people look when they travel. At the Ritz in Paris, people coming and going look awful. Poor grooming, crinkled hair, and sweatsuits. It is not the best of times."

Galanos admits, "We're living through an age of vulgarity. But I don't think elegance is out. I think there will always be elegant men and women."

LILACS, LINCOLN,
AND LITTLE LAKE

June 1993

A memorial service is often difficult to attend. Not so, the one for Marie Maazel. The gathering at Heinz Chapel celebrated her life, and I think we all grew to know this woman, who died at age ninety-seven, as the young Marie's story began to unfold. If I was sad it was because I hadn't known her longer.

I can still smell the lilacs. The pulpit was banked with more lilacs than I have ever seen in one place. They hung on the chapel's pillars and on the sides of the pews, tied with purple satin ribbon. They were her favorite flower.

The music, played by former members of the Pittsburgh Youth Symphony, which was her passion, now musicians with orchestras in Pittsburgh and Boston, and by her son, Lorin, and her grandson, Ilaan, filled the chapel with the sounds she also loved. That included an old recording of an aria, "Pourquoi Me Reveiller?" from Massenet's *Werther*, sung by her favorite tenor, Tito Schipa. The scratchiness of the recording was there as proof it was old and proof it had been played many, many times.

Her daughter-in-law and grandchildren, and her husband, Lincoln, were escorted to their seats and then came that marvelous voice of the Pittsburgh Symphony's Michael Lankester, who read a poem her husband had written and dedicated to her. There was so much love in the chapel that evening. It was only enhanced by Lorin Maazel's reflections about his mother as he painted a picture of a spirited young woman. She was known to ride horseback on the beaches of California and Big Sur. And then," her son said, "my mother found a man in whom she recognized great gentleness...my father, Lincoln."

I had known Marie Maazel for many years and probably met her when she was in her '60s, long after her horseback-riding days. I had never seen her as the young woman her son described but he expressed it so beautifully. I felt I was being introduced to her for the first time, and appreciating her more and more.

My connection to the Maazel family has been through Lincoln. We performed in plays together at Little Lake Theater in Canonsburg, Pennsylvania, before I knew that he and Marie had raised a music prodigy named Lorin, now music director of the Pittsburgh Symphony. I also never knew Lincoln had musical talents and was an excellent teacher. As Lorin stood there playing a favorite Tchaikovsky opus on the violin, accompanied at the piano by his son, I recalled the famous Maazel photo seen around the world of Lorin conducting a symphony orchestra as a young lad wearing short pants. He started to play the violin at age five. And now he was playing his mother's favorite music, and her grandson was to play another favorite, the Chopin Waltz in B Minor.

Marie Maazel attended almost every performance of a play at Little Lake in which her husband played a kind of Damon Runyan character, complete with striped suit, spats, cigar, and a Brooklyn accent. She smiled with pride. Her husband loved acting, and she stood right beside him, loving it too. I was thinking about that as the classical music surrounded us and I recognized how she embraced all that faced her in her long life. Until the service I had not seen Lincoln for a year or so, but he had written to me in response to a note I had sent when I learned that Marie had died. He was staying with his son's family in Monte Carlo and the note he sent to me was touching. "She remains in our hearts a great lady," he wrote of his wife. "The outpouring of love and sadness has been overwhelming."

It's rare and wonderful to see a love like theirs. I am honored to be even remotely in its shadow and to have been touched by them in my lifetime.

PROM DATE WITH THE MAESTRO

June 1996

Last weekend I thought I had died and gone to heaven. That might sound familiar to anyone of a certain age who attended the Marvin Hamlisch Prom Night concert at Heinz Hall. Standing there in front of our great symphony orchestra with permission to reminisce about my senior prom? Wow.

If you grew up in the '30s, '40s, and '50s, the years Hamlisch featured musically in the Pops concert, you know what I'm saying. If you loved to dance, even better. We danced a lot back then. The music was incredible. The memories are forever.

This invitation to be "prom queen," based, I am sure, on my nostalgia reputation, was like stirring up a repressed addiction. It's an addiction to big band music with heart and soul, songs with lyrics you can still pull out of your head. That's no easy feat since I will be attending my fiftieth high school reunion next summer. You can do the math.

Standing in front of all those musicians, men in white dinner jackets and women wearing white blouses and dark skirts (one musician wore her '40s poodle skirt) and with Hamlisch in tails at the podium, well, is it any wonder I was in heaven?

A bit of background: Several months ago I was asked if I would take part in the Prom Night which was Hamlisch's idea to close the 1995-96 Pittsburgh Pops season. When they asked me to be the prom queen, I thought they had made a serious error. Did they know how old I was? I agreed but was puzzled. A few weeks later I was sitting in my living room munching something or other, watching a movie on TCM. The phone rang. I answered. "Hi. This is Marvin." Did I know a Marvin?

"It's Marvin Hamlisch." Oh, *that* Marvin! Well, what would you do? I muttered and stammered and then he began to tell me his plan for Prom Night. All I had to do was jot down a few words about prom memories. I wanted to gush and go on and on about his music and the concert he conducted for Barbra Streisand, but I didn't.

When he hung up, I still didn't understand my role in the evening's events, but I soon learned when I attended the one and only rehearsal for the show…which was having its first performance that very night. "Marvin flies by the seat of his pants," I was told. "It always turns out just fine." Nervous? You bet.

I sat at Heinz Hall and spotted Joe Negri's (on guitar) familiar face. He would be featured, sitting in with the orchestra. Me, on stage with Joe Negri! There was a professional actor, Laurent Giroux, brought in to play a high school principal, and he would introduce me. Hamlisch misses nothing.

Then I sat and listened while the featured professional group, The Platters, rehearsed their familiar numbers. I sat in the back of the hall and watched every performance after my bit was done on performance nights. I had my own dressing room, with my name on the door! I was in show business!

After the rehearsal I headed to Lubin & Smalley because I knew I had to have a gardenia corsage if I was going to a prom. I asked Sid Rosen if he had gardenias in his shop, figuring it might be a flower nobody sees these days. I was right to ask. But he did have one…just one. And then he made a call and ordered three more so that I would have a fresh one for each performance. Judging by the applause and smiles (and a few couples dancing in the aisles), I wasn't the only one transported back to a simpler time. None of us "died," but for a couple of hours, those of us who remembered the past were in heaven.

A BLASS FROM THE PAST

September 1996

Maybe it was a scoop. Maybe a bit of history. Maybe a bit of farewell. Maybe all of the above.

I was heading for Bill Blass's Sutton Place, New York, apartment, going past the streets where I had lived briefly in 1951, before, quite frankly, I knew who Bill Blass was.

But this time as I peered from the taxi window, seeing familiar sights between Second and Third avenues at 57th Street, where the EL had once hung above the streets, I was feeling just a bit sad. I had read that Blass might be writing his memoirs soon. That's a sign of closure.

Nobody recognizes changing times better than Blass, who arrived in New York from Indiana in the early '30s, and went on to become one of America's best-known designers.

The door to his apartment was ajar, and I heard the familiar voice call out, "Hello, Barbara. Come on in." We've talked many times the past thirty-five years, but I was glad to hear him say my name. He'd be embarrassed to know this, but when he came here for the opening of the new Saks Fifth Avenue store nineteen years ago, he greeted me with great confidence. "Hi, Susan. Good to see you." It happens. It helps me keep my head straight, quite frankly.

But I like this man. And I sense an end in sight, an end to a spectacular design career. He's committed to a collection for fall '97, but after that, who knows?

Blass came to Pittsburgh five times to be honored at the much-missed Horne's Symphony Gala. The fifth time was the twenty-fifth and final gala. He always drew a crowd. Customers loved him.

The melancholy in his musings is easy to spot. It's in his constant questioning, as if he is seeking confirmation…is it time to go?

We began to talk about his New York, back in the '30s.

"I love the city, understand. I thought then it was the most exciting place in the world. It's still exciting. I like the fantastic energy. That's still here. I adore the museums and the restaurants."

His tone changed. "But now you must be conscious of crime, constantly. Today you find small courtesies rare. The city is dirty, and there are so many homeless people on the streets. It's unattractive, unlike Milan and Paris, which are beautiful. I think it's for young people."

He paused. "I know the way I talk is a sign of age." He brought up age more than once. He's seventy-four. He asked my age, as if seeking a kinship.

"I spend most of my time in the country, with my dogs," he went on. He mentions his pets often—always has—and he talks about them as one mentions family. "They're a Lab and a golden," he adds.

What does he do in the country? "Well, I am usually awakened at 5:30 a.m. by my one dog who sleeps with me. We go for a walk. I eat dinner early and I go to bed early. I don't cook much anymore"—he makes a mean meatloaf—"and I never had time to take up golf, so it's a fairly quiet existence."

Don't feel sorry for Blass. He lives extremely well. He happened to mention he recently had lunch with Nancy Reagan. His country neighbors are other designers, Oscar de la Renta and his wife, Annette; Carolyne Roehm; musician Peter Duchin and his wife, Brooke Hayward; and Henry and Nancy Kissinger.

"Nobody wants to look rich these days," he mused, "and yet people are richer than ever. It's not lack of money. It's attitude. People don't want to be noticed in their clothes."

He's not going on the road any longer to visit major stores and boutiques. Although exclusive stores like Martha in New York (out of business) helped bring him great success, he sees America today as "violently over-stored."

"I stopped doing trunk shows because I was snapping at my clients. You can tell when someone is enjoying what they do. I sure wasn't. I love the idea of making the clothes. That hasn't changed. But then, I never want to see them again.

"It's not public relations or publicity any longer," says Blass. "It's advertising, page after page after page, like Ralph, Donna, Calvin, and now Hilfiger. They spend anywhere from $40 million to $70 million in any given ad campaign. My spending $10 million is insignificant in that market."

He was shaking his head and shrugging his shoulders as he looked at his spectacular view of the river. "It's not the same," he said.

He looked out at the bridges and the sunset. He sighed. "'I'm not the same."

CHICKEN SALAD FOR THREE

December 1996

Gertrude Miller has so many stories she wants to share, she asked me to visit her in Apollo. We would have some lunch—her own chicken salad—and just talk. I wanted to meet her whether she had stories to share or not.

Mrs. Miller is one of the reasons I like what I do. I am privileged to meet so many real people, many who inspire me and many who remind me there is so much that is good in this world. We all need to be reminded. It is easy to become discouraged with today's world, its morals or lack thereof, its violence and dependence on material things.

Mrs. Miller is a woman who remembers when gas tanks on the North Side blew up in the mid-1920s, and the explosion broke the windows of her house. She recalls her mother's lovely lace curtains dangling on outside wires on Duquesne Heights.

"People in Downtown Pittsburgh saw this great ball of fire, and they thought it was the end of the world," she recalls. And in some ways it was, perhaps, the beginning of the end of a world she knew.

Mrs. Miller has written to me through the years. I have always been impressed with her thoughts and her lovely stationery, which tells you this is a woman of grace and caring.

It was a glorious afternoon for my journey, which seemed appropriate. I wasn't even sure where Apollo was, but I headed in the easterly direction of Holiday Park and Armstrong County, took Route 380, and got lost.

I wonder what draws me to people who were already in the working world or raising families when I was but a babe in diapers. Gertrude Miller had worked for Agnes House, who had a downtown dress shop (long gone). It was Mrs. Miller's interest in fashion, and thwarted career as a fashion illustrator, that caused her to write to me some years back.

She married and raised her children, but she still thinks about "*What if?*" There are examples of her painting talent throughout her house, with fruits and flowers painted on trays and tables and china.

Since suffering a stroke a few years ago, she doesn't think her fingers are as deft as they once were, but looking around her home, in this mobile park developed by her son, Meredith, I can see she has the touch, and I am sure she still has much to say with a paintbrush.

And while she wanted to share some stories of family and unusual meetings and marriages and coincidences, I found Gertrude Miller herself to be my column inspiration because there she was in front of me. She was real.

"It gets lonely, as you can see," she said, "being way out here in the country." But her home is cheerful and bright and filled with pictures of family.

I could help her with nothing. She sat me down in her "music room," which has a small antique record player as its centerpiece, and as she busied herself in the kitchen with the chicken salad she had made, I looked at the table she had set. There were the lovely white linen luncheon cloth and napkins, sterling silverware and blue-and-white china, and on a nearby tray, a decanter of home-made thirty-five-year-old cherry liqueur, and thimble-size, sterling-trimmed glasses. All the niceties of times past.

She had greeted me holding a cane, and there was a walker on the porch, but inside she used neither. "I hope you can put up with my slowness," she said as she looked for an appropriate container for the flowers I had brought.

I knew she loved flowers because of her stationery. Bright red geraniums were bending toward the sun at one kitchen window. Her dessert plates were decorated with handpainted flowers. I just knew.

We talked of many things. She doesn't watch much television. She did not plan to vote, but would have voted for Ross Perot, she thinks. She always wanted to travel the world on a steamship. She once had a dog she loved named Topsy who had a puppy they called Turvy.

She was born in 1903. Start counting back and you realize she is ninety-three. My own mother, had she lived beyond age seventy, would have been two years younger than Mrs. Miller, and oddly enough, her maiden name was Miller.

On the drive home, I thought about my mother. It was as if she and I had just had a visit...and as if we three had shared chicken salad. It was very comforting.

CHANGE OF HART

April 1998

She was so pretty. And so talented. Her name was Dolores Hart, and her movie file bulges with typical studio promotion pictures with actors like George Hamilton, Stephen Boyd, and Jeff Chandler. Back in the early '60s, she was headed for stardom when, abruptly, it ended.

Why it ended is a touching story that came to mind when I was watching *Entertainment Tonight* a few weeks ago. They were interviewing the young woman who had given Elvis Presley his first movie kiss in *King Creole*. The year was 1958. The actress was Dolores Hart.

The question she always got in interviews about her movie career was, "What is it like kissing Elvis?" Was it embarrassing to be asked such a question? Was that to be her legacy? She was amused when I asked her that recently, and not the least bit shy.

"I think the limit for a screen kiss back then was something like fifteen seconds. That one has lasted forty years." And she chuckled a bit at the memory. There is far more to this beautiful woman than that kiss, believe me.

I wrote to her after seeing her that night on *ET*. My letter simply stated how good it was to see her looking so well and, obviously, expressing delight that her decision to leave the movies, a difficult one to be sure, had turned out so well. She was happy. It had been the right thing to do.

How could she give up her dream of being an actress? Her answer was simple. "How could I not?"

She called me a friend, but we had been out of touch for close to thirty-five years. Our connection was through my job as a reporter for the *Pittsburgh Press*. She came here twice, the first time in 1960 to promote the film *Where the Boys Are*, and each time it was a pleasant meeting. I felt comfortable talking to her.

But on her second promotion tour to Pittsburgh in 1963 she was a different person, distracted and introspective. I noticed the change but didn't think much of it, until I read a few weeks later that she had left the film industry to enter the monastic life at Abbey of Regina Laudis in Bethlehem, Connecticut.

Four years later, in 1967, I heard from her again. She explained why she had seemed pensive and withdrawn during our last meeting, although by then I knew. I wanted to do a story about her new life, but she wasn't ready for that.

"It wasn't that I didn't like the media. I found it stimulating. And I wasn't running from it. But when you decide to do this you must give all of yourself, just as I gave all of myself when I was an actress."

The letter she wrote to me as Sister Judith, before her final vows, detailed to some extent the anguish she was experiencing at that time. "It was really a nightmare," she wrote, "in that I was so absorbed in coming here at the time, my heart was hardly able to contain anything else. Naturally it was also the one thing I could not speak about, so my memory fails in recalling much about that era."

I more or less forgot about Dolores Hart after that, but now she was on the phone, still showing the gracious manner she had as an actress, but more than that, willing to answer all my questions, friend to friend.

There is a reason she is suddenly "out there" and it has to do with a CD called "Women in Chant," which features the choir of Benedictine nuns at Regina Laudis singing Gregorian chants. Sales benefit the work of the abbey.

Mother Dolores Hart, O.S.B., is credited with the cover photo of the nightblooming Cereus (as ethereal as Georgia O'Keeffe's two Jimson weeds in oil, to my eyes), and she is also part of the choir, although she never considered herself a singer. For that matter, she never saw herself as a nun.

"It was not a lifelong dream," she said. "I did not grow up wanting to be a nun. I wanted to be an actress. If it had ever been suggested I would one day be a nun, it would have been the last thing on my mind. It was a million-to-one shot I would ever be a nun.

"As a child I was precocious," she said. "My parents married when they were sixteen and seventeen and both were beautiful people. Moss Hart offered my mother, Harriett, a contract but by then they had me, and my father, Bert Hicks, a bit player, definitely a Clark Gable type, had movie offers so we moved from Chicago to Hollywood. I was a Hollywood brat. We lived in Beverly Hills and I used to visit the lots with him. He had a bit part in *Forever Amber*. I always wanted to be part of that life."

Her life took another direction, however, while she was appearing on Broadway in *The Pleasure of His Company* in 1958 with such renowned actors as Cyril Ritchard, Cornelia Otis Skinner, Charles Ruggles, Walter Abel, and former Carnegie Tech student George Peppard.

She had already been asked to re-create her role in the film version of the play and she was excited about that. Then, one night Debbie Reynolds came to see the play and took notes during the performance. Dolores Hart realized she was not going to be in the movie and it was a big blow to her. But other things were also happening.

"A friend suggested visiting this very tranquil place in Connecticut one weekend and it was Regina Laudis Abbey," she said. "After that, whenever I was on the East Coast, I would go there. I began to notice each time I went it was becoming harder and harder to leave. I had this feeling I was home."

A few years passed and she continued doing movies until one titled, *Lisa*, which dealt with the Holocaust and experiments done on prisoners at Auschwitz, sparked something inside her. "It affected me so deeply, and more and more I found myself drawn to the abbey."

When she entered the abbey, Sister Judith was selected as her name because she was, after all, starting a new life. A new name seemed appropriate, but when she made her final vows she changed it to Sister Dolores. It was also a wish from her mother, to keep the name Dolores. "Hal Wallis wanted to call me Susan when I started my movie career," she recalled, "but I was under age and my mother would not hear of it. She wanted me to be Dolores."

Would Hollywood ever see her return? The odds, she says, are a million to one. But those were the same odds she would ever become a nun.

A CASE OF FAMILY HISTORY

I would have liked Aunt Myrtie. I never knew her. But recently I found bits of her life in a faded and dilapidated suitcase.

In it are letters from Helen Keller, her signature carefully printed in blue-ink block letters, outlined in yellow. There are notes from the White House during the terms of Roosevelt and Coolidge. I sense a bond.

Do you ever wonder how you became who you are or if knowledge of your ancestors might show you why you are doing what you are doing? A son or daughter might follow in a parent's footsteps career-wise, almost in natural succession, but when you are separated by generations, it is indeed odd to discover a relative you never knew about, and then to learn that her interests were so close to your own.

I sat down at the kitchen table with my late Aunt Edna's son, Jazz, and the object of our attention was an old suitcase with ripped sides and a rusted handle that he had found among his mother's belongings after she passed away in January at age ninety.

He said much of it was news to him as well, especially since most of the clippings and photos in the suitcase were of a woman we never knew. We weren't even sure how we were related as we read the papers, but we finally decided Myrtle Miller McMaster was our late grandfather's sister. Our mothers were two of thirteen children fathered by Elwood Miller and Elizabeth Cleaver.

I never knew either grandparent. In fact, my mother never spoke of her parents. She was sent to a foster home when it became too difficult for her mother, a nurse, to raise all those children.

Now I was learning about someone who would have been my

mother's aunt, someone my mother probably didn't know at all. She certainly never mentioned Myrtie Miller to us as we were growing up. My sister and I only learned we had all those uncles and aunts when we were about sixteen and eighteen.

So here was all this information about Myrtie, and some of it was mighty impressive. She obviously married well. Alexander McFall McMaster was a physician, and they lived in Washington, D. C., for some time.

Aunt Myrtie corresponded with the White House, it seems. There are several letters on White House stationery, answering inquiries from her, when Franklin Roosevelt was in office.

She was interested in a variety of causes, and she was religious and caring. There is a card from President and Mrs. Coolidge thanking Aunt Myrtie for her expression of sympathy to them. It is dated 1924, the year their son died.

She was born in 1878, and her maternal grandmother was Barbara Ann Lightkep, born in 1811. That would have been my great-great-grandmother, who could have been someone I was named after, although the woman my mother was raised by, whom I knew as Nana T, also was named Barbara. She was Barbara Tomlinson. I was never told for whom I was named. I have no idea where my middle name, Louise, came from.

But I was learning more than I had ever known about a relative, even a distant one—primarily that Aunt Myrtie was an actress, traveling with the Riggs Comedy Troupe in 1908, and a writer who had many of her articles, poems, and songs published.

Among the papers in the suitcase were 1909, 1913, 1925 and 1926 copyrights from the Library of Congress for periodicals, a book, and songs with words and music by Myrtie Miller McMaster. She seemed to do it all.

I would love to have heard the song titled "I've Lost My

Thimble" and another titled "Tuck Me Away on Thy Bosom, Mother."

When she married Dr. McMaster, their names were often on the society pages. In 1926, the distinguished jewelers, silversmiths, and stationers, the Bailey, Banks & Biddle Co. of Philadelphia, invited them to be represented in their volume of *Two Hundred Armorial Families of America.*

She often wrote letters to the editor, one in which she expressed dismay at the bobbed hair trend, stating "it lends an appearance of coarseness, grossness, and mannishness that should be entirely foreign to the feminine feature." Ouch!

In 1927, Aunt Myrtie copyrighted a piece called "The Gateway to the Physical," in which her lead sentence refers to a woman's uterus. Shocking! That must have turned more than a few bobbed heads.

I instinctively like her, having only this cardboard suitcase of papers as an introduction. A life summed up in tattered and yellowed clippings and photographs in a cardboard suitcase. Sometimes it comes to that. I'm glad it found its way to me.

STANDING OUT IN A CROWD

June 1999

Bess Flowers was what Hollywood described as an "extra" in films. More succinctly, she was a "dress extra." That was in the Hollywood of long ago.

Flowers has grown on me, and I have to admit I found myself through the years seeking her out in crowds, particularly party or nightclub scenes in movies made in the '40s, '50s, and '60s. I don't know why. I only know I'm still doing it in TV reruns.

My interest wasn't overpowering at first. I just found myself muttering, "There's that woman again," when I would spot her. It meant nothing to anyone but myself. Then I began looking for her without realizing it.

"There she is." I'd poke my friend as we watched the Saturday matinees.

"Who?" she'd ask.

I don't think I ever answered. But it was "that woman."

I learned Bess Flowers's name when the movie *Midnight Lace* was being publicized in 1960. Philip Katz was the local movie publicist, and he contacted Bob Ungerfeld at Universal's New York office. A still photo from that Doris Day movie showed the actress, and within days we had her name. Katz wrote to her to see if a phone interview was possible, but sadly, Flowers never responded. Who knows? Perhaps she wanted to remain an unknown, although how many actresses do you know who feel that way?

My interest waned some through the years because I wasn't seeing her as often. Enter AMC cable network. Several months ago, I was watching *The Young Philadelphians* (1959), starring Paul Newman, on AMC, and *The Manchurian Candidate* (1962).

There in my living room I said it again. And again. "There she is," I said out loud for no one to hear except my dog. "There's Bess Flowers."

So I'm off and running again. I contacted scriptwriter Thom Thomas in Los Angeles, who sent me a printout of all the films in which she had appeared, beginning in 1931, from the *Motion Picture Almanac.* She was in such films as *It Happened One Night* (1934), *Cass Timberlane* (1947), *The Bad and the Beautiful* (1952), and *Rear Window* (1954).

Unfortunately, I also learned she died on July 28, 1984, at the Motion Picture & Television Country Hospital in Woodland Hills, Calif. She was eighty-five. Born in Sherman, Texas, she stood five feet eight—another reason I admired her as a teenager who stopped growing at five feet ten. She started in notable roles, it said in her *Variety* write-up, in many silent films, and later as a bit player.

She was married twice, first to Cecil B. DeMille's assistant director, Cullen Tate, and then to William Holman, studio manager at Columbia. She had a daughter from her first marriage.

Her bio states she developed a reputation as "Hollywood's best-dressed extra," and I was told many such extras in those movie days were chosen because they could provide their own wardrobes. She always looked stunning.

I had a feeling she probably made a good living, and she never had to learn lines. But that's not entirely true. In one of the last scenes in *All About Eve* (1950), she speaks to Anne Baxter after Baxter receives an acting award. A full sentence, no less. In *Imitation of Life* (1959), she can be seen taking a curtain call in an early scene with Lana Turner, and later, after the cast awaits the newspaper reviews, she bids "Goodnight, George" to her host. I wish she had known she had a fan in Pittsburgh.

MEAL FEEDS MEMORIES

October 2000

Our Isabel. How do I begin to tell you about her? She worked for us, and she was part of our family, living with us for seven years when I was a little girl.

We all shared a single bathroom, her room was next to mine and my sister's, and she was our friend.

Several weeks ago, I received an e-mail from Terri Tobay. My eyes began to tear. This was Isabel's daughter writing to me.

As much as Isabel had meant to our family, when she left us I was maturing just enough to be selfish and concerned only about what was happening in my young life. I was then fourteen. I lost track of her. I never forgot her.

Isabel met her husband, Joe Boskovitch, while she lived with us. Like Isabel's father, Joe was a coal miner. She left when they married. That was 1943, during World War II.

I did not know she was just fifteen when her parents, Anna and Andy Urban of Edenborn, patients of my father, brought her to stay with us. I was seven; my sister was nine. Many families needed the extra income, and children went to work. Isabel had six sisters.

She started at $5 and then $7 a week and managed to contribute to her family and also pay for her own clothes.

Isabel says she cried for a week when she left home, but she soon became comfortable with us and visiting her family on weekends. It couldn't have been easy.

This was someone who watched me grow, who comforted me the day my sister cut off my curls when we were playing barbershop.

Isabel was usually the first person to arise at our house, getting to the coal furnace to stoke the fire, then fixing our oatmeal after an almost daily ritual of baking bread. I see the loaves so clearly on the top of the radiator, in their pans swathed in blankets to make the bread rise.

She still lives near Uniontown, Pennsylvania. After her daughter's message, we arranged a visit.

She told me I had hated oatmeal. "You only liked spaghetti, and apple pie with milk." All is still true.

My clearest memory is of Isabel's neatness. Her room, her bed, her clothes, her hair—precise and neat. Did she ever get angry or rant and rave? Not that I recall. It was not her nature.

My sister and I would sit on her bed Saturday evenings as she dressed to go to town. We would watch her set her hair (with bobby pins), and we would help her select the dress she would wear. She loved to go shopping on Uniontown's Main Street. Those were the days when the streets were alive with people and stores.

Isabel liked to go dancing. She met her husband at a dance at the Polish Hall. And she liked movies.

She now has macular degeneration of her eyes and had a stroke five years ago, but as we hugged, as I tried to clear the lump in my throat, she rubbed her hand through my hair and said, "Oh my, your hair is so short." She remembered long curls, of course. She could not see my features, just the outline of my face, but as I listened to her, I felt she saw me clearer than most.

She has had a hard but wonderful life with a son, Nelson, twin girls, Terri and Kathy, and another daughter, Jackie. There are twelve grandchildren (another is due) and five great-grandchildren.

Her house is so neat, I could have guessed our Isabel lived there. She loves to point out the things Joe built in their house. He worked hard all his life and suffered a great deal from the cancer that took his life ten years ago.

"At the end, he couldn't talk or move, but when I went to kiss him, he puckered," Isabel said with great delight and laughter.

"I think maybe I saw your first pucker with Joe," I said. I thought I was confessing after almost sixty years. My sister and I used to wait for her to come home from a date and peek to see if Joe kissed her, then run giggling to our beds.

"Oh, I knew someone was on the stairs," she said matter-of-factly. We hadn't fooled her at all.

She remembered that my father would take all of us for ice cream on hot summer nights. My parents bought her her first wristwatch. She still has it.

Isabel, Terri and her daughter, Erica, and I ate lunch, and of course, Isabel had made the noodles for the wonderful chicken soup. She had also baked the bread. Her illnesses have only slowed her down; they have not kept her from her kitchen.

It was a feast. The meal fed my memory. I saw my family's kitchen.

Terri knows of her mother's big heart. Isabel helped her raise her own two children, three and seven, when her husband was killed by a drunken driver in 1984.

Today is Isabel's birthday. Tomorrow is my own. Her best gift? Having her family around her. Mine? Knowing she was once part of mine.

LAUGH LINES

June 2002

When I learned Phyllis Diller had decided to retire from touring, I was relieved for her. No more shabby dressing rooms, no more technical difficulties, no more disappointment with an audience. But I was also sad.

She will be eighty-five on July 17. She knew it was time to retire, but she still loved making people laugh. But when I observed her dark dressing room a couple of years ago, when she donned that wild wig, painted her face, and climbed into her pointed-toe satin booties, I had to wonder why. Why did she keep going?

She was at Carnegie Music Hall in Oakland for a benefit. That's a pretty nice place onstage, but when I climbed the steps to the dressing room after her show, I felt she deserved better, even if it was a light bulb with higher voltage. She was eighty-two. Some respect was due.

The audience hadn't been particularly receptive either, and she knew it. She was not surrounded by an entourage of people waiting on her. She sat in front of her mirror and, I thought, seemed more than a bit lonely. I don't know what she was paid for that performance—maybe it made up for the gloom.

She did talk immediately about the audience "not getting it." I laughed heartily, but many people around me did not. She didn't miss it. Humor has changed. You have to rant and swear, get down and get dirty. My feeling that night was that Miss Diller was too good for us. We didn't deserve her efforts. And maybe it was time to say adieu.

A year before that she was at a casino in Jackpot, Nevada,

doing two shows a night and we did an interview by phone. Why was she there? Wasn't she weary?

"I'm funnier than ever," was her reply at the end of our chat. "Whoops, gotta go. It's show time."

Forget that she had heart surgery and "died" three times on the operating table just three years ago. She has a pacemaker, but who would know? It seems an engagement in Palm Beach a few months ago in which the mike wasn't working convinced her it was time to quit. Simple as that. Or maybe it was also a dark dressing room. Perhaps the audience there "didn't get it."

For a woman who was planning a barge trip and a biking trek through Europe at eighty, it wasn't surprising she was gutsy enough to keep touring for so long. She has come to Pittsburgh many times since I first met her in the '60s. She says she is leaving show biz to spend more time painting and to write an autobiography.

She's an original. She took many of us with her on her journey as a stand-up comedienne and we have laugh lines to prove it. Still, it was heart which made her a star.

HANDSOME AND NICE—
A POTENT MIX

October 2002

I remember John Weitz very well. First of all, the men's fashion designer who died of cancer recently was so darned handsome. He was easy to remember.

As a woman on the fashion beat covering both men's and women's collections for many years, I could get giddy facing this tall, dark, and handsome man with what sounded like a British or Oxford accent. He knew he was charming. That was okay. And he was nice to listen to. That affectation in his speech matched perfectly his very deep voice. He was dreamy to look at, with chiseled features and a movie star aura. He even married an actress, Susan Kohner.

At my age (I had just turned seventy-three) and his (he was seventy-nine), the obituary columns hit home more often than not. We know too many people. At my recent high school class reunion, I read the names of sixty-four deceased classmates and that included nineteen more than at our reunion five years ago. I see all of them as young, and that memory is a good one, even though none of us had really begun to live our lives as we passed each other in the halls of Uniontown Senior High School fifty-five years ago.

Recalling connections to various people, famous or not so famous, is what we do as we get older. Memories can be sad but also sweet. Weitz was not a bosom buddy of mine. He was part of a business I got to know well for more than thirty-five years. He had a period of strong recognition, in part because of his good looks, and also because of his marriage in 1964 to Miss Kohner, who was much younger than he and who starred in the five-hanky movie *Imitation of Life.*

Weitz was always available to editors. After his runway shows, he would stand on the stage and tell you why his clothes worked for the average man, especially price points. He liked to take off his own sport jacket and roll it into a ball to illustrate what men would do when they traveled. They would stuff the jacket in the overhead bin, take it out, and wear it upon arrival at their business meeting. No wrinkles!

He spent time on boats and in sleek racing cars, looking tan and a bit like Cary Grant under stylish aviator sunglasses and his own outerwear, brightly colored seaworthy parkas or turtleneck sweaters under leather jackets. Every man might not look like him, but they sure wanted to. Designers laughed, but Weitz was onto something, and he was his own line's most effective salesman.

I had met him and seen his New York shows several times. When he came to Pittsburgh in 1971, I wanted a one-on-one interview, and he agreed. It was February 3. Why do I remember the exact date? My son was born that day. My noon interview with Weitz, scheduled weeks before, of course, was not to be. I had gone to the hospital at 2:30 a.m. and Drew was born at 7:36 a.m.

Weitz sent flowers and a baby's silver rattle, and he also called me at the hospital later that day. He told me that my becoming a mother was far more important than interviewing him and he promised me much joy in years to come. He was a proud father of young children himself. At moments like that he came off his fancy pedestal and I saw just a regular dad and a very nice man. Yes, a very nice handsome man.

So, I liked the man for personal reasons but I also thought it was fun to watch many of the designers who laughed at his kitschy approach to fashion in his early days. They never considered him one of them, but his success has left many of them in the dust, this man who had his name on such ordinary things as socks, ties, and underwear. He marketed overseas, one of the first to realize the potential. Weitz was never Cardin or Armani but he found his niche. He had a long run, even if couture wasn't mentioned with his name.

Later he began to write novels and they were scoffed at as well. But he was having fun. Maybe he was just too good-looking to be taken seriously. We couldn't get past those chiseled features to see the real man. I saw a hint of that man on a February day thirty-one years ago. His prediction about my joy as a mother was right on the money. I've never forgotten it. I won't forget Mr. Weitz. How can I? I still have the silver rattle.

A PINCH OF LOVE

May 2003

Just about anybody could gather mushrooms, cheese, spinach, eggs, flour, and seasonings, roll some dough, and create a pie. Ah, but would it have loving hands, lots of laughs, hugs between stirring and slicing, and of course, the "Wednesday is pie day" tradition?

There are cooks, and then there are cooks.

The two women I observed early one Wednesday morning are the Tenuta sisters, Linda Ruggeri and Edith Monsour. For the past twenty years, they have been arriving each week at Ruggeri's Market, 5878 Northumberland Street, Squirrel Hill, to bake the pies, which have a quiche-style filling but a lattice-top crust.

The pies are the specialties, but also bubbling on the stove weekly (and made with loving hands) is a huge vat of spaghetti sauce as well as the makings for rice puddings, two other originals sold in the market by the owners, John and David, who are Linda's sons.

There aren't many Wednesdays they miss in any given year, and this is the market's twentieth anniversary.

Much of the joy was taken from the weekly activity three years ago when their sister, Evelyn Belotti, died. The three sisters had done everything together, and that included baking spinach pies. It's not the same without her, the sisters agree. There's an empty space. Still, "We try to keep going," says Edith.

John, David, and another brother, Mark, who died in an automobile accident in 1986 at age twenty-two, helped their father, James, at Ruggeri's Meat Market on Freeport Road, O'Hara Township, when they were growing up. A fourth brother, Jimmy, was the only one who decided the food business wasn't for him. He has a hair salon in O'Hara.

I arrived at 7:00 a.m. just as truck deliveries were being made to the store. The sun was up, but barely.

Linda, 78, and Edith, 82, drive in from O'Hara every week. Edith still lives in the Tenuta family home in Blawnox. Their mother came here as a bride from Italy in 1920, and their father worked in the mines in Harmarville.

We got our coffee and headed for the basement kitchen, where everything is as neat as a pin. I pulled up a stool as the two women donned their aprons and began the four-hour ritual. The pastry shells were already made and waiting for the filling about to be put together.

"We would talk nonstop, even if you weren't here," said Edith. "I love coming here. I always look forward to our pie day, although it was nicer with the three of us."

Linda, a widow, looked at her sister and nodded, her chin quivering just a bit as she thought of Evelyn.

"Here, you start with the garlic," she said. Within minutes, Edith had sliced a garlic head for the spaghetti sauce, and then two large baskets of mushrooms that would then be lightly sauteed in a huge skillet for the pies.

While I was paying attention to Edith's deft chopping of the white mushrooms, Linda had quietly begun the rice puddings. Every burner was going. Talk about aromatherapy! Filling for the pies was taking shape in a container the size of a laundry basket, as cheddar cheese and spinach, onion, and the cream mixture were stirred.

I was watching but truly didn't realize all they were accomplishing as we chatted about the good old days, when life wasn't quite so complicated. Edith was already rolling out dough and cutting it into narrow lattice strips to create the pies' top crusts. It was as if each one knew exactly what the other was doing, and it was all perfectly timed. After twenty years, not surprising. Linda would fill the shells, then hand each one to Edith, who would top them with lattice strips.

"It just makes it prettier than a solid crust," she said. She returned the pies to Linda, who brushed them with whipped egg and then put them in the large oven.

Fresh basil went into the spaghetti sauce, which would cook for three hours. It was breakfast time, but at that point I yearned for a dish of pasta. The rice pudding was finished in an hour, poured into containers, and sprinkled with cinnamon.

"We're always mentioning something our mama used to do," said Edith, "and we talk about Eve and how much we miss her, and our grandchildren, the next generation. It's nonstop."

But will a younger Ruggeri generation continue this tradition? I don't think the sisters expect that pie day will be forever. But for now, as long as these sisters can laugh and have a story to tell and be with family, it's never boring.

The pies are ready and sealed in Saran wrap. Another Wednesday, another forty pies.

The garnish? A generous helping of love—you can never add too much. After all, it's a Ruggeri family recipe.

HIS BARK IS WORSE
THAN HIS BITE

February 2004

How do you describe someone who defies description? The late Dr. Jack Knochel meant too much in the lives of too many people not to try. Because there was no death notice, many people will be getting the news today in this space.

If you'd ask most people who knew Dr. Knochel to describe him, they might think for a minute and then rattle off words such as "unusual," "one of a kind," "class clown," "borderline brilliant," "peculiar." But always they'd add, "An excellent, caring veterinarian."

For all the years I carried my pets over his threshold at Pittsburgh Animal Hospital on Washington Boulevard in East Liberty, I did not know his first name until February 4, when I learned he had suffered a fatal heart attack. He had just turned sixty-one.

He was just Dr. Knochel. He was my vet. My quirky vet. I say that with affection.

About seventeen years ago when I took my eleven-year-old Springer spaniel, Beau, to the hospital for a shot, he said, "Want another dog?"

"No, I don't think so. I don't have a bed or puppy food or ..."

"Don't worry. Take him for the weekend. If you don't like him, bring him back."

He was a Lhasa apso, just a few weeks old. I named him Wicket and loved him for seven years.

What I realized sometime later was that Dr. Knochel, in his own way, was preparing me for the loss of my spaniel, who was getting old. I would lose Beau within the year.

It's not just that I did not know his first name. I barely knew the man, even though my visits to his hospital with the first of four pets began in the '70s. But if you met him, you'd never forget his crooked grin, his sense of humor, his storytelling, his "unusualness." He marched to his own drummer, that's for sure.

His coworkers at the hospital, who will keep the hospital open, are really mad at him. They are mad because they cared about him and he paid little attention to himself. He had had a heart attack thirteen years ago, and still he smoked. He didn't eat healthful food.

His life was wrapped around his "beloved animals," those he cared for as patients and those he kept at his farm in Sewickley. In addition to his eight dogs, there were cows, squirrels, ducks, goats, sheep, deer, a llama, a peacock, and a mountain lion named Samantha he had raised from a cub. His nephew, Tommy, is arranging for new homes. It isn't easy.

They were pets. They all have names like Bubba, Tipper, Baby, Sweetie, Roxie, often named after people he knew. His coyotes were Willie and Monica. That was his sense of humor.

Of his eight dogs, he seemed to favor Butchie, the Jack Russell terrier that would take naps with Dr. Knochel in his office.

His only sister remembers her brother raising a calf he named Holly in his kitchen. He was fascinated by animals, she said, ever since he was a child.

When we made decisions to put any of my dogs to sleep, he was there to assure me it was best. Never emotional, but there. He didn't cry with me. His quick and often aloof manner might have made him seem uncaring. It was just his way. I have since learned he would not watch films such as *Bambi*, *Born Free*, or *Old Yeller*. They made him cry. He would hate that we know that about him.

And yet—and this is baffling—he was also a hunter. Along with snapshots of many of the pets he has cared for, a picture of a caribou he bagged in Labrador hangs on the office wall, next to a picture of blue-eyed Samantha, his lion.

He didn't care what anyone else thought. This is a man who also cared for a disabled younger brother who lived with him. For years he gave his time to free rabies clinics.

"He loved to tell stories. We never really knew if they were true," says Jessica Folner, who has worked for him the past six years. "I never knew anyone like him. He was great to work for, although not everybody could have. You had to understand him."

Maribeth Hook, another staff member, tells this story: "He had this intuitive way. When I had to euthanize my Great Dane, he was patient with me but then had me stay while he did a Caesarean on another dog. I helped bring the puppies around. It was a very thoughtful way to help me get through my grief. For me, he was a very special person."

That was the complexity of the man. Even those who worked by his side admit he was an enigma. Peculiar, odd, and eccentric to some. Also compassionate, generous, and caring.

We should all leave such a legacy.

WADE WAS MEANT
TO BE SARAH

May 2004

Do you see people in everyday life you would like to meet or know more about? I have felt that way for several years about a former cashier, now in customer service, at the Murray Avenue Giant Eagle in Squirrel Hill.

Her name is Sarah. That's what it says on the ID badge she wears on her green smock. I can remember when it said "Wade."

A few years ago I was checking out my groceries, looking down at my checkbook when I automatically asked, "How are you, Wade?"

Softly but firmly, she replied, "It's Sarah."

Somewhat startled, I looked back at the face, then the badge, and indeed, it was "Sarah."

Wade Smith had become Sarah Wade-Smith. It was a gradual gender change that most regulars at the store had surely been aware of, myself included. But I wasn't prepared for the name change, even though I was aware Wade's hair had been getting longer, makeup more obvious, polish on the fingernails, and more feminine jewelry.

Wade was now Sarah.

Ever since, I have wondered about her life, how she is treated, what makes her tick.

Like many transsexuals, Wade realized when he was a young boy that he liked to wear women's clothes. But also, like many in his situation, he fought it and tried to conform. In high school, where it really got rough, he went out with girls, played soccer and softball, and joined ROTC, all in an attempt to fit in.

"I was always teased, I guess, for my effeminate ways," Sarah says, "and what we do is try to find ways to endure, to fit in. I was always looking for literature to help me understand my feelings. I developed a great imagination, and I read a lot. But there comes the day you hit the wall and you can't pretend any longer just to please others."

The full name change came in 1999, and she selected the name from a book she had never read, *Sarah, Plain and Tall.* She kept Wade as a family connection to her grandfather, whom she loved very much.

So, what's it like going from Wade to Sarah?

"Liberating," she says, as we sit having lunch and a three-hour conversation at Eat'n Park. She was born in Tennessee and majored in public administration and history at the University of Tennessee. She feels she should be doing more than working at Giant Eagle the past ten years, but she is comfortable there and loves the diversity of the people she meets. She has often thought she would like to run for public office.

"I was always an outsider. Even my interest in science fiction was different. My one brother [she has two sisters and two brothers] told me he often got beat up because I was so weird when we were younger. The isolation is the worst part of trying to fit in and be what you are not. But no matter, I was always the odd one."

She says that matter-of-factly. She just didn't understand why she was an outsider, why she wasn't like everybody else, especially boys. She told me she is fifty, adding quickly, "But I look younger, don't you think?" Just like a woman.

Complete sex-change surgery was out of the question because of the cost. It has taken a lot just to afford electrolysis and hormones, Sarah says. And she loves clothes.

"I spend most of my time in the store uniform, so I don't buy many clothes, but I look for pretty things. I also like makeup, which surprised me. I found myself enjoying putting it on and I think the reason for that was I had to look in the mirror. And I would often think, gee, I'm pretty."

She goes to a salon for her haircut and color but otherwise maintains the chin-length bob herself. "Oh yes, I use rollers and all that. It takes time. And I love big, outrageous jewelry."

This day, however, she wore pretty but inconspicuous rings and a silver chain with a single rhinestone drop around her neck. Her denim dress had a square-cut neckline and short sleeves, revealing smooth, hair-free arms. She's formidable at six feet tall and a dress size 22. Finding fashionable clothes is a challenge.

There's the name-calling, too, but she has tried to develop a sense of humor about that which, with support groups, helps her through the rough times.

She once took a martial arts class as a precaution.

"You know, as a guy, I was simply wearing armor," she says, "and the day I finally came to work in women's clothes I was ecstatic. I always felt unattractive as a man. I also felt vulnerable. As a woman I have much more self-confidence and I am often even more aggressive."

Talking with Sarah is a delight. She is well-read, funny, loyal to her friendships. She has been in love and not had that love returned, and she knows that pain. She knows how to be a friend. She knows depression. She talks about her church and she quotes well-known writers with assurance.

The best part about being female? She thought for a moment. "I like the way women relate to each other. I have learned to value that intimacy—and girl talk. Men don't have that."

Is Sarah happy? Despite the rough times she talks so openly about, she seems to be. "I'm certainly happier than when I was growing up. Than when I was Wade."

HEART OF AN HEIRESS

February 2005

Maybe in your lifetime you have met someone you would like to have known better. I felt that way about Cordelia Scaife May, a woman alternately described as funny, articulate, and generous, as well as reclusive and publicity-shy. And now it is too late. Mrs. May died January 27 at age seventy-six.

But maybe you can know her better. She was just like you and me in so many ways. Please don't laugh, although she might find that funny as well.

I had exchanged notes the past several years with the heir to the Mellon fortune, a philanthropist who quietly gave away her money, and on her terms. It would not surprise me to learn that she wrote notes to many people if she had something to say, but knowing her reputation for not talking to reporters, I was all the more surprised when one day I received that first small envelope with her return address on it.

Never mind all that has been and will be written about her, some of it speculative, some of it gossip, some of it flattering, and some of it not.

In most of the obituaries in the country's leading newspapers, her name was in the headline as "banking heir." They dutifully reported that she was annually on Forbes' list of wealthiest Americans, ranking number 363 last year with a net worth of $825 million.

There are other reasons to attract the curious, juicy stories, including ill-fated marriages to Herbert A. May and Robert Duggan. And there was the long estrangement from her younger brother, billionaire Richard Scaife. I did not know these aspects of her life. I'm sure she had good, loyal friends who know her far better than I. It's just that I am glad I knew her at all.

Mrs. May wrote to say that she enjoyed my columns. They often reflected a more innocent time, where she, too, wanted to dwell. I was surprised to realize that, because she was known as a voracious reader of far more serious stuff. When she was going on vacation one year, she told me she was taking "stacks and stacks of books."

In spite of the unhappy childhood recounted in various memoirs, she savored and shared a few memories, usually the simplest of things, such as going to the movies on Saturday afternoons. She delighted in an incident at a movie theater when she kicked off her shoe and it fell over the balcony into the audience below. As teenagers do, she said, she and her friends couldn't stop giggling.

When I wrote about having a teddy bear as a child, she sent me a current snapshot that showed her hugging her favorite teddy bear. I was touched. Later, she sent me a snapshot of two black bear cubs on her front lawn, so close she could almost touch them. She loved nature, loved living in her wooded surroundings in Ligonier. That's the kind of correspondence we had. Nothing deep. Just nice. And surprising.

Each envelope that arrived made me smile. The stick-on address label, just like the ones we receive from various groups hoping we will send a donation, was printed with the name of one of America's wealthiest women and a rural box number. How cool was that?

She invited me to lunch one day at the Pittsburgh Athletic Association, where she always stayed when she came to the city for meetings with her Laurel Foundation staff. I was nervous, but she was easy to talk to, and we laughed a lot during lunch. I think she sought humor and loved telling funny stories.

I understood her better after reading a story in the *Washington*

Post in which she said, "I don't remember any laughter in that house," referring to growing up in a home in which she was raised mostly by governesses.

Mrs. May always commented on my photo notecards, a hobby I began about five years ago, so I invited her to an exhibit of my photographs at the Twentieth Century Club in 2002. She sent regrets, saying she had to be in Dallas that week.

But then, the following week, she told me she had visited the Twentieth Century Club after a meeting and before driving back to Ligonier, and she said she especially liked the quirky shot of two rather round-figured sunbathers whom I had likened to "a set of salt and pepper shakers." That, she said, made her laugh. Her notes always referred to laughter. "Have a happy, healthy New Year...with lots to laugh about" or "with plenty to smile about," or my favorite, "with frequent splotches of fun."

In her final note in December, she said my Christmas card with a photo of the tree and skating rink at PPG Place was on her mantelpiece. She loved Pittsburgh. That pleased me. I couldn't know it was to be her last Christmas.

What she didn't love was seeing her name in print, so I hope I am forgiven. I wanted others to know her beyond "banking heir." That shouldn't be her legacy. Cordy May was a real person—and in many ways, just like you and me.

AUGUST IN OCTOBER

October 2005

I was among several hundred people who attended August Wilson's funeral at Soldiers and Sailors Hall in Oakland last week. With the funeral in the birth city of this world-renowned playwright, I expected thousands to attend—not the few hundred that I observed.

I was compelled to go, as if he were my friend, as if I had known him since childhood. I did not know him. And yet, I did know him. He shared his life and the lives of others with me through his poignant, angry, humorous, yet delicate pen, scratched on a long series of napkins and notepads through the years. I was grateful the funeral was in a public place, open to strangers like myself who wanted to pay their respects.

It was like witnessing the ending of what we can only hope is a beginning of understanding, which will continue because he has told his stories so well. I wasn't alone in not knowing the man or his family. Many of us who were there, black and white, didn't know him.

Our Hill District, the background for much of his writing, is the neighborhood through which I would ride the 82 Lincoln street car up Centre Avenue during my early years working in Pittsburgh, back in the '50s, and yet, until Mr. Wilson took his pen to paper, I knew nothing about its history or the people who lived there.

He would have been about twelve when I was beginning my life in Pittsburgh as a young reporter. He was somewhere out there, an unknown, as I traveled through his neighborhood day after day.

I took a bus to Oakland for the funeral, fearing parking would be a problem. I had been aware of a petite, older black woman getting on the bus, wearing a little hat on her softly curled gray hair, walking slowly as she balanced herself in the aisle of the bus. I smiled at her and guessed we were headed to the same place as we got off at the same stop. But we walked separately. She said she was to meet someone. However, once inside the auditorium, we found ourselves seated near each other as we awaited the services, and we began to talk.

Her name is Alma Burgess. As inspired as I was with the service, the singing of "September Song," the "Spiritual Baptists," and Wynton Marsalis playing "Danny Boy" like I have never heard it before, it was meeting this tiny articulate woman that brought it home. I will remember her for a long time.

She, too, had never met August Wilson. Together we observed the people walking in. Much like me, she was impressed that actors Charles Dutton, Ruben Santiago-Hudson, and Phylicia Rashad were there. We both gasped at catching a glimpse of S. Epatha Merkerson, who plays the chief on TV's *Law and Order*.

"Today's my birthday," Mrs. Burgess said after we began to chat. "I'm eighty-six." I told her mine was coming up—today—and I would be seventy-six.

"My friends couldn't understand my getting on a bus on a rainy day and coming here on my birthday," she continued. She smiled and said quite simply, "But this is where I wanted to be."

That was it. We were two women, one black and one white, with totally different life experiences, or so I thought. She has lived ten years longer, so she knows more than I do. But she expressed just what I was feeling. This was where I wanted to be on this chilly, dreary day, celebrating a life that should touch us all.

Mrs. Burgess worked in the city's public schools for many years, but her own children had attended Phillips Exeter Academy in New Hampshire, the Ellis School in Shadyside, and Harvard University. She had worked with good and bad students during her career, and she wanted her children to have the best education possible.

Different races, and yet we were sharing this day because we just had to be there, honoring a man neither of us had ever met.

I thought, this is what August Wilson will be doing as long as we have his plays and the legacy he left for us. If only we can continue to talk, to learn, to understand, and to accept our differences. In many ways, we are so much alike. That's what we'll learn.

It's unusual to be humming a song from a funeral service, but "September Song" still goes round and round in my head. The lyrics set the mood: "The days dwindle down to a precious few."

And so they do. For all of us.

A LIFE GOES UP IN SMOKE

June 2006

In 1969, just two years after Wilhelmina Cooper started her own modeling agency, I was privileged to interview her in New York City at a trendy spot called Sign of the Dove.

She had been one of the most recognizable models of her time in the late '60s and early '70s and she was considered the last star of the couture era in modeling. She had appeared on 255 magazine covers, including twenty-seven on *American Vogue*, a record.

Her more than ten years as a model were the years I became acquainted with the fashion industry as a young woman. That face and swan-like neck were so memorable. I was trembling at the thought of being opposite that famous face.

I am reminded of that day because of a dining experience I had recently. I was seated with a friend in the smoking section (just three tables) of a restaurant. We were lucky to get a table on a weekend night in town, so it didn't bother me.

When a young man at one of the tables asked if we minded if he smoked, I really didn't mind. I did, however, want to tell him not to, for his own good health. He said he was twenty-nine, somewhat addicted, and I suppose he thinks he has plenty of time to quit, or might not at all. I'll never know. It made me think of Wilhelmina, someone who we thought had it all. She died in March 1980 at age forty.

Unlike Dana Reeve, who died this year of lung cancer and did not smoke, Willy, as she was known, puffed away continuously, even during our lunch.

I would learn years later that this noted beauty, born Gertrude Behmenburg, also suffered as an abused wife of an alcoholic husband, the late Bruce Cooper. Their daughter, Melissa, told Michael Gross (author of *Model: the Ugly Business of Being Beautiful*) she believes her mother chose to kill herself with cigarettes instead of facing, and fixing, her horribly imperfect life.

Even casual, she was the personification of a model as I imagined one to be. They aren't always.

Her modeling fee, $60-$75 an hour, was top dollar at the time and she earned between $60,000 and $70,000 a year. Some models today earn that much in a weekend.

She had ordered eggs Benedict with a tomato. She told me tomatoes were her weakness, and she obviously had never tired of them.

She said she had weighed 159 pounds when she started to model. She lost about ten pounds when Paris discovered her, and eventually found she felt her best energy when she was around 126.

"I was always the heaviest model," she said. And she always had to wear a girdle. Who knew? But back then, many women wore girdles.

"I could appear slim by the way I posed, but I became determined to lose weight, and I simply began to starve myself." She wasn't exaggerating as she shared her "diet" secret as a model with me this hot summer day. Daily she drank a half glass of tomato juice, black coffee—and smoked cigarettes. Then more coffee, and more cigarettes.

Every Wednesday she would allow herself a small bowl of tomato soup, and on Sundays a tiny steak and one piece of Melba toast.

"I'm still young, [she was thirty]" she said, "and I am used to hard work, which is why I started the agency." She told me that day her husband was "the big boss" and the brains behind the business.

A few years before our interview when she was in her prime,

81

I had seen her posing at the fountain at New York City's Plaza Hotel, surrounded by cameras and stylists and a gawking public. She was a true mannequin, standing on that wall in a gorgeous gown. I was late for my appointment, but I became a gawker, too. I couldn't help it.

Ten years after this lunch, Willy would succumb to lung cancer. She would have turned sixty-seven last month. The agency, with new owners, still bears her name.

THE NOSE KNOWS

April 2008

Do I remember Charlton Heston? You bet I do. In a strange way, he was like family. When I read of his death at age eighty-four, I immediately reminisced about our "connection."

During the years I worked as a reporter for the *Pittsburgh Press*, and later at the *Post-Gazette*, I met many celebrities and was fond of many…but more so with Heston.

That's because we looked alike. Well, that's what I was told, and when I look at a picture I have standing with him, in profile, during one of his visits here at least forty-five years ago to promote a film, I think to myself…yes, we are dead ringers for one another…by a nose.

As a female, I don't think being told one resembles an actor such as Heston would be considered a compliment. He has been quoted as saying, "I have a face that belongs in another century." That makes the vanity in me wonder about our look-alike declaration.

Strong-boned and muscular. His face was even "hawk-like." Those aren't the body descriptions a woman might deem complimentary, but because it was Charlton Heston whose profile was in sync with mine, I am proud to acknowledge it.

I don't recall the exact year this came about, but I am going to guess early '60s. Why I was sent to interview him at a church on the North Side, I also don't recall. But there we were and it was not a long chat but he was very gracious, and nice enough to pose for a photo afterwards.

I was always star-struck, and certainly was on this occasion. He was a very popular actor at the time.

Then, within an hour, I was on my way to another interview,

quite different from this one with a movie star. I also wrote about garden clubs at the time, and this woman grew beautiful orchids. Of course, her name escapes me, but what happened when I arrived at her home was uncanny.

I walked through the door and she stared at me, then apologized as she remarked, "Did anyone ever tell you that you resemble Charlton Heston, the actor? You could be brother and sister."

Then, with my jaw agape, I told her I had just been with the actor who was in town promoting a film. She said she had no idea, but still, "You do look alike."

I went back to the office, wrote my story, and then, a few days later, the photographer gave me a copy of the picture he had taken of me with the actor, both of us in profile, looking off into space.

We did, in that photo, look as if we could be related, although I'm not sure anyone else would see it. Still, a definite possibility. And while my jaw is strong and a wee bit square, like his, it definitely is the nose which is the likeness. Mine is not a small, cute nose…nor was his. Hawk-like seems fairly accurate.

I would interview him again a few years later, this time in a room at the William Penn Hotel. I remember it vividly because he wasn't wearing shoes and as we talked he sat cross-legged in a chair and played with his toes! This was Moses (his most famous role), playing with his toes! And telling me his costar in the movie *El Cid*, Sophia Loren, was a "double helping of a woman." Think about it. He was telling me she was voluptuous in a very nice way. I always loved that quote.

And then I told him about that unusual day a few years before, after our interview, and the orchid lady's observation. He immediately stood up and took my arm and guided me to a mirror in the hotel room.

"She's right," he said. "I can see it, can't you? It's the nose."

I had never liked my nose, although I have learned to live with it and never once considered a nose job. My features are not cute, my nose is not cute as a button. I don't dress cute.

There was another interview with Heston in 1965 in New York City and the discussion was the influence in fashion from his current film, *The Agony and the Ecstasy*, in which he played Michelangelo. In spite of his masculine image, he didn't mind wearing an artist's smock. But he did opine some clothes made women look ridiculous.

Once again, Sophia Loren's name came up. "She is one of the beauties of the world," he declared, "but she often wears the most appalling hats. I like turbans and I liked them even before I played Michelangelo."

Did he have a fashion extravagance? Yes. He said he was addicted to silk shirts.

Oddly enough, just a few days ago I was watching *The Greatest Show on Earth*, surely one of Heston's most memorable movies. I was remembering all of the above, plus how nice he was. And how young he looked in that film.

I was remembering watching him on the late Peter Jennings's show, his wife Lydia beside him as they told us he had symptoms of Alzheimer's. It seems this "relative" of mine lost his memories long ago. I still have mine and I wanted to share them once more.

"I've had too much music to really appreciate rock and roll. Some of it is nauseatingly exciting, but most is just nauseating. A ballad might be harder to get off the ground, but it stays up longer."

—Billy Eckstine, 1959

"Don't worry. I won't desert the average woman, because this is where this type of clothing at a moderate price is needed the most."

—Calvin Klein, 1970

"I'm just trying to play understandable jazz. I never play a song twice the same way, but I try to get as close as I can."

—Erroll Garner, 1959

"Unisex? I think women should look like women and men should look like men."

—Nancy Reagan, 1968

"Whenever I make a personal appearance with Benji (there have been four in the role), animal shelter adoptions go up. That's what I want the films to encourage."

—Joe Camp, Creator/producer/
writer/director of the Benji films, 2004

"Fashion is made by fashionable people—not by designers."

—Halston, 1973

flowers

theater

classical music

photography

nostalgia

weddings

letters

cities

dolls

food

jazz

family

dance

fashion

dolls

taxicabs

flamingos

film

movies

radio

children

design

sandwiches

What

BRINGING UP BABY

September 1976

Three days after my son was born, well-meaning friends were advising the best nursery school. Pros and cons of those schools, the Montessori method, kindergarten techniques, and allotted hours for TV viewing followed close behind in bringing-up-baby conversation...on the way home from the hospital, as I recall.

After a month or two, while I was mashing bananas and pouring his formula, colleges were even bandied about.

The decision to take each day as it came seemed like a good idea. Otherwise, I might throw in the towel before he was out of diapers.

So far away? That little bundle weighing in at 6 pounds, 11 ounces, started school this week. He now weighs in at 47 pounds.

My advisers were right. I know it was just yesterday I scoffed at school advice. Surely it wasn't five years ago.

"The time goes so fast," acknowledged one friend who has raised four children.

"They aren't little very long," chimed in another.

Those mother-child emotional embraces on the first day of school have been subjects for photographers for years.

I doubt they can be appreciated until you send your own little one off to school that very first time.

There are so many firsts recorded in childhood.

In baby books, the first three years are almost day-by-day diaries as to weight, height, cute sayings, first step, first word, first visit to Grandma's, first solid food, or first high temperature.

After first birthday, first tooth, first Easter basket or visit to see Santa Claus, you move from infants' to toddlers' clothing departments, and notes jotted down become less frequent.

Some people claim the beginning of school is the time you let go…irrevocably.

To say it doesn't wrench the heart is to deny heaven and earth, the fact rain is wet or the sun is warm.

To watch a little boy walk away from you into a school building…on his own more than any time thus far in his young life…it is a memory, indelibly etched.

If all has gone well, a youngster has started breaking away even before school.

Being sent off to birthday parties, weekend stays with grandparents, playing at someone's home other than his own, learning not to cry each time he is left with a babysitter.

Children are being prepared to be on their own as soon as they draw a breath, turn over in their cribs, feed themselves, or crawl to a desired destination.

But school…that first day…it is special. He doesn't know it, of course. You do.

It begins a long stretch of years of learning, achieving, competing, winning, losing, making friends, creating memories.

The snapshot you took that first day will be tattered and torn by the time he is a senior. Chances are you will save the little shirt he wore and it will be put with the booties and sweater and bonnet he wore when you brought him home from the hospital…when school days were centuries away.

Is it possible?

Memo: Send for college applications today…well, it's only kindergarten…tomorrow will be time enough.

RIDE ON THE WILD SIDE

April 1990

Cab fares aren't bargains in New York City, but they used to be. You could get in a cab with $3 and get just about anywhere.

But the New York drivers are still part of the "character" of the Big Apple. Sometimes it's good, sometimes it's bad. But always interesting.

What strikes me is the change in the drivers. The majority used to be from Brooklyn, or at least longtime "New Yoorkahs." They almost always engaged in lengthy chatter about the city, the world, the mayor—anything at all, even when you preferred silence. But you relied on their knowledge and experience driving in Manhattan.

You might even meet a budding actor. Former Pittsburgher Charles Grodin drove cabs during his lean days pursuing acting in New York.

On a recent trip I encountered three drivers who left indelible impressions on me. One was from India, another from Pakistan, and the third was from Greece. All lived in Queens.

The youngest of the three, from India, gave me the ride of my life from uptown to downtown. I am often in awe of drivers in New York, and more amazed when I get where I'm going without so much as a scraped fender. I don't think I have ever been so frightened, not only by his speed but his daring, in darting in and out of traffic. Much like a movie chase.

When we reached my destination, he looked in the rearview mirror and said, "Lady, you okay?"

I had literally been gripping the arm rests and bracing my feet against the front seat during the entire ride, and he knew it. I might even have let out a squeal.

"I know I drive too fast. My wife tells me all the time."

She must wonder each day if he's coming home.

He has been driving for eight years. He grew up not far from where I was going, below SoHo, but it was not a good neighborhood. He wanted better for his daughter, so he lives in Queens.

I liked him. I hope he is still alive. I hope his daughter is never his passenger.

The Pakistani driver kept calling me "Ma'am" and saying, "Please," a word you don't hear often. He was delightful, a student at Columbia University. It was difficult being in a strange country, he said, and he had come all by himself three years ago. He admitted it was frightening to drive a cab in New York. A week earlier two men got in his cab and put a gun to his head and told him to keep driving and not to stop for anything, particularly a policeman.

"Yes, please, I did what they say. I thought they might kill me."

He said they were dividing a large stash of crack into dozens of individual bags to sell on the street as he drove them around. "Yes, please, there was nothing I could do," he kept saying to me. "Earlier tonight a young girl, maybe fourteen, got in my cab and offered me sex to get money for drugs. Yes, please, it is terrible. We do not have this at home."

The third driver, the Greek, was talkative and friendly, but I soon found he also was much too personal in his conversation. Was I married? Where did I live? Why didn't I move over so he could see me better in the mirror?

I kept laughing. He said he was married and had two children. I told him I could be his mother and that I was anxious to get home to my husband. I lied. I had been divorced many years.

Suddenly he said, "I want to put my hand on your knee."

I kept laughing. He was a pleasant enough hustler, but I was getting nervous—and I pretended to be working on some papers the rest of the ride.

"You are busy? I won't bother you," he said as he realized I was trying to concentrate on my imaginary work. I was drawing doodles on the notepad and praying we were headed to the airport. We were.

"I still want to put my hand on your knee," he said as we headed up the LaGuardia ramp. "It's good luck."

"I don't think so. It's a bad idea," I said, seeking the sign for USAir as my savior as we pulled up to the curb.

"What would your wife say?" I asked.

"Are you crazy? I wouldn't tell her," he said, laughing.

Whew. Made it. Or so I thought. I was distracted for one minute and darned if he didn't reach back and put a strong handclasp on my knee. I didn't feel threatened. I was just amazed at this guy's nerve.

"I did it," he called back as he took off, waving merrily. "Have a good trip."

If I had been in Pittsburgh I would have reported the young man who drove so fast, and also the man who put his hand on my knee. For some reason, in New York, it's part of the package.

TABLE TOPS NOSTALGIA

December 1990

At my house we don't see the top of the dining room table from now until a day or two before Christmas.

It's where I wrap my presents and address my greeting cards. But from the moment we burp and excuse ourselves from Thanksgiving dinner, it's no longer where we eat our meals. I clear the table and bring up the box of ribbons and paper from the basement.

Actually, it's my tiny nod to nostalgia. I happen to have the dining room set I grew up with. It is scuffed and, in some places, could use a good resurfacing and polish, but it has so many memories.

My parents moved to a smaller apartment once my sister and I were on our own, and my mother didn't want to part with the dining room furniture. She had no room for it, so it went into storage. I knew she hoped my sister or I could use it some day, but you know how young people are. My sister never had a dining room and to me it was "too old-fashioned." At that time I think I was into all that teak and sleek Scandinavian furniture.

Of course, it didn't compare to the carved pieces belonging to my parents. But what did I know? Finally, about sixteen years ago, when I had my own house with a real dining room, I gave in — really to make my mother happy. I was not convinced this was great stuff.

In the end, it has become my contact with the past, and I treasure it every time I sit down or open the drawer to the china closet where our scarves, hats, and mittens used to be stored. I open that screechy drawer, and I see my sister and me grabbing our mittens and racing out of the house to school or to build a snowman. But the table—ahhhh, that's where I see my mother.

She put fantastic meals on it through the years, but it was her wrapping regimen that is the most memorable. She sat at that table and wrapped the most beautiful packages, taking so much time to select a ribbon, make a special bow, neatly tuck the corners, and every so often she needed my finger to hold the ribbon while she executed a bow.

She, too, covered that table from the time we cleared it from Thanksgiving dinner until Christmas Eve.

It's strange what eventually makes a memory. It's never the big things. This table, for instance, has been touched by most of the people I hold dear in this world. Favorite aunts and uncles, old boyfriends, Mother, Daddy, my sister, good friends, my son, his friends.

The table is there every day of the year but this is the time I sit there and share special moments with my mother.

Our lives did not go without sad times and misunderstandings, but thank goodness the best of times come back as I sit there, remembering her generous nature, her beautiful smile, and those talented fingers wrapping treasures for friends and family. I've never mastered her technique with ribbon.

The joy of the holidays revolves around family. That's true even when some loved ones are no longer with us. Day-to-day living builds the memories we keep forever. And they can include something as basic as a dining room table.

IF ONLY I'D KEPT THAT

Do you ever turn masochistic and think of all the things you wish you had saved? It's like sticking pins under your fingernails. It hurts.

We tend to toss the good things and hang on to the totally useless. As soon as we toss out something, it becomes a treasure we should have kept. That's why most of us are up to our eyebrows in "things." Still, we try to weed out nonessentials from our homes, garages, refrigerators, and closets. The idea is to make way for new nonessentials we can weed out later.

Lots of people are neat. Some are obsessively neat. But the average person probably saves and saves, then has a sudden urge to get rid of things when one more pair of stockings won't fit in a drawer or there's zero storage space left in the basement.

Getting ready for Christmas is the thing that usually inspires me to clean house. I get in those boxes and see all the things I never put out for display but keep putting back for the next year. And usually the boxes are wedged between other boxes of unused items.

I have pieces of fabric from three chair covers I've used and tossed the last eighteen years. I have bits of wallpaper I'll never use, and that the former owner of the house had saved from the '40s. It takes up space in my attic. It's crazy. Sure as I write this, I'll throw it away and have use for it the next day.

There's always superfluous stuff that just grows—like every vase in which you ever received flowers. Most are ugly. But there they are, lined up on a shelf like soldiers awaiting inspection.

Then there are the treasures you save for just so long and then decide to toss or give away. I am reminded of my Shirley Temple doll. Had to be an original. I say that without giving away my age, but a few flicks of your fingers and you'll know—I'm older than thirty.

Anyhow, I don't remember what my sister and I did with our dolls, but they were beauties. And a dear friend of the family, Margaret Ritenour, who was the high school sewing teacher, made us the most beautiful doll clothes every year for Christmas. Our Shirley Temples had incredibly stylish wardrobes. That might be what led me into this career, who knows? I particularly remember Shirley's brown snowsuit with the fur-trimmed hood.

The dolls are valuable today, although we played with ours so much they were well-worn after a few years. We brushed and washed and curled the hair. Mine got bubbles on her face when I tried to "warm" her in front of the heater after a bath. We enjoyed the dolls. That was the important thing. Still, I wish I had saved her, just to look at.

But that's how our basements, attics, and stairwells get so full.

As soon as I gave away a book about Jacqueline Kennedy Onassis, I needed it to find out who designed the gown she wore when she married John F. Kennedy. When I tossed an old issue of *Vogue*, I needed it within days for a story about James Galanos. I could have given my late mother's eyeglasses to the Pittsburgh Guild for the Blind to pass on to those in need, but I got rid of them without knowing.

In grief you usually throw out things you should keep. It's best to wait a while, until you can think straight. I wish I had not gotten rid of my engagement ring, but divorce emotions raged.

Now I think about tagging things I hope will be kept when I am no longer here to protect them. Like my Mickey and Minnie Mouse dolls, which are at least fifty years old and from the first issue by Walt Disney. I have been reading that teddy bears can have real value in mint condition. Ha. That's the catch. If you had a teddy and dearly loved it, chances are it is missing some of its plush, maybe part of its nose, just from being squeezed so tight over a period of growing-up years. I hope there isn't a parent alive who would keep a teddy from grubby little fingers, just to keep it in tip-top shape for eventual cash value.

But I sure do wish I had my Shirley Temple doll...and my dollhouse, my train, and the board for it under the tree. And the Pucci print blouse I gave away after twenty-five years. Finally, it's back in style.

I have a sweater I bought in Copenhagen twenty-four years ago. I never wear it but it hangs in my closet. Why? Even when I gather clothes for the homeless shelters, I pass over that sweater.

Toss it and you'll want it tomorrow. You always throw away the wrong things, just as you always hurt the one you love.

S'WONDERFUL,
S'MARVELOUS

July 1997

Every so often I ask myself—and maybe you have as well—what couldn't I live without? Or, at least, what would my life most notably miss if I no longer had it? I am not including people we love. They are the most precious, of course. And I know we need food and water to survive physically. But the soul, the spirit, the heart . . . they need music.

What good is a nourished body without a nourished soul? An artist, a poet, an actor might feel differently, but even in those areas, music often makes the words and emotions mean even more.

When the music swells as it did when Tara came into view in *Gone With the Wind*, or when the airplane flew into the clouds in *Out of Africa*, I am putty in a screen composer's hands.

Music weaves a spell and, I think, brings out the best in us. I have measured many things to music and what it means in our lives. I have considered those things which please me and give me joy and peace, including beautiful colors.

What would the world be without color? What would it be without sunshine, without cool breezes, sunsets to make us gape, or sunrises to make us squeal with delight? All the meaningful things in life, at least to me, wonderful as they are, are only magnified by music. It is the one thing that can make me feel a full range of emotions. I find music is the thread of life, tying me to the beginning and the journey from there to the present.

Who said, "Music is the sound track of your life"? It's accurate, but not just your life...life itself. To hear music echoing throughout your house via stereo speakers, to choose love songs or religious songs, songs with whimsical lyrics or lush sonatas, Pavarotti or Bernstein, jazz vocals or the violins and orchestrations from Jackie Gleason . . . what joy.

I like to tap my feet at jazz jam sessions. I remember hearing Illinois Jacquet at the Syria Mosque years ago and being blown away. I used to put opera singers' records on our old Victrola, wind up the side mechanism, and play them full blast in our attic. Yes, I'm that old.

I studied piano and did recitals, but I don't have even the slightest gift for music, except for appreciating it. In that I am stellar. I was nurtured with music. I can't get in tune with the MTV crowd and all those groups with weird names, but you see, I don't need them. There's more than enough out there to send me reeling.

In the '40s, we would stretch out on the floor of our sunporch to hear the bands from hotel ballrooms on radio late at night. Musicals, of course, were a favorite entertainment at the movies when I was growing up. They made me every inch a romantic, not a realist, but I'm not complaining.

The story told in *Shine* inspires us, but it is the music which takes us to that other level. We feel our emotions ten times over because of the music and the manner in which it is played.

Whether the real David Helfgott plays as well as others isn't the point. If he moves us as an audience, what does it matter if he misses a note? Many musicians hit all the right notes and are critically acclaimed, and yet, they don't move us.

Whether music makes you feel melancholy, silly or serene, riled or romantic, the fact it makes you feel at all is its importance.

From lullabies to school bands, vocal renditions to instrumental geniuses; from coaxing music from a cumbersome cello to a table of metal rods—with which Lionel Hampton makes pulses pound—making music is a gift.

So music, maestro, please.

POT ROAST AND
PEARL HARBOR

December 1997

December 7 will live in infamy, as President Roosevelt said when he announced the attack on Pearl Harbor in 1941.

It isn't that what I was doing was so memorable. I was just doing the everyday kind of thing American families do at this time of year. It was a Sunday, and I was twelve. I can't remember exactly what we were having for dinner, but it was probably a roast or a leg of lamb. Sunday dinner was always special.

Normally we sat around our dining room table, using cloth napkins, my father at the head of the table slicing the meat. Mother would be at the other end of the table. The dog would be under my chair, ready to catch whatever I would want to share. When I think of that day, I automatically smell a roast and mashed potatoes and gravy. It's a safe guess, being Sunday.

After Thanksgiving, the dining room table became the Christmas wrapping table, and December dinners would be served in the kitchen.

That day, my mother was at the table doing her magical thing with gift wrapping. When she was wrapping something for us, she would alert us to "stay out of the dining room," and we would get all giggly trying to guess what she was going to give us.

So I place her in her usual place. My father, I think, was upstairs. My sister and I were in the sunporch, a room at the front of the house where we often did our homework and listened to the radio, which was console-style with a record player on one side.

So, there we were that Sunday afternoon. As a family we were together, and there was a security in being in a warm home and planning for the holiday. We never dreamed that our lives would change that day—forever.

I don't remember the exact words as the program we were listening to was interrupted. I do remember calling to my parents to come and listen, because I didn't understand what I was hearing. War? We're at war? It was something out of a movie. It wasn't real life. It wasn't the life I knew, which was protected and safe and almost always predictable.

There wasn't a serious thought in my head, other than washing my hair and calling my best friend to talk about the movie we had seen the day before. We always went to the movies on Saturday afternoons. I was in junior high school. Boys were great but only to climb trees with or exchange marbles and comic books. But that was just beginning to change.

Now we all gathered around the console to hear the news. My father leaned in to hear it better, to understand and translate what it meant as the familiar voice of our beloved president, in his slow and precise manner of speech which we knew so well from Fireside Chats, told us we were at war with Japan.

The most vivid memory I have is the house itself on that day. The comfort and the uneventful life we had led there were about to change. Shortly my father would be called to duty, first stateside and then to the South Pacific, and even then as he left us for the first time ever, we had no idea just how great the change would be. He would be gone for five years. I was seventeen when he came home for good.

It wasn't only us, of course. Everyone in the country was reacting to the news with disbelief. It was so far away. It was so removed from us. And yet we were at war, and the subsequent years would show us what it was to have a household minus a father, and minus many of the things we were so accustomed to having as rationing began.

Today marks fifty-six years since Pearl Harbor, and it's a Sunday, which makes the memory even stronger.

My father came back to us, but he was never the same. My sister and I grew up and became teenagers during the years he was gone. Mother changed, too, and she became our anchor, but she was so lonely. It couldn't have been easy.

Now I sit at my mother's table, the very same one, which is already piled with wrappings. I carry on that tradition she started, but I'm not nearly as talented. What is the same is I am wrapping presents for people I love, as she did for so many years. I will sit there today, wrapping and remembering my family and feeling closer to them than usual. I'm sure of that.

A roast is in the oven. It's December 7. And that's the way it was.

FLOWERS ON A BLANKET

April 1999

We are in such turmoil around the world. We have come off a year filled with distrust, deceit, degradation, and frustration. The incidents at the White House cloud our thinking and make us curious about what is true and what isn't. Should we or should we not be dropping bombs on Kosovo? What is right? What is wrong?

That's what haunts me today, even though I want to sing praises and rejoice on an Easter Sunday. I smile at little girls and boys in their Easter finery. They represent such hope for tomorrow.

Spring buds appear, and the smells of new earth and blossoms greet us. Wake up and smell the roses.

There have been so many disagreements since President Clinton and NATO ordered the bombings of Kosovo. Many say, "I don't care what goes on over there. It means nothing to me. Those people mean nothing to me. It's none of our business."

Most of us don't even know where Kosovo is. We are wrapped up in our own existence. Let's face it, we have it pretty good. We eat our pizza, enjoy March Madness, complain about our government, and often have nothing better to do than fidget with computer software, complain about Mariah Carey's choice of dress for the Academy Awards, have another pizza, or strap on our rollerblades and head for the park.

A single photograph among all the horrible pictures of war and destruction affected me deeply, more than any affirmation from Washington. I cut it out of *Life* magazine last October. I tucked it in a book, and from time to time when I would open that book, there was that beautiful child, eighteen-month-old Valmir Deliaj, lying on her back, blood and dirt on her face and in her dark curls, a floral blanket covering her dead body and the bodies of her murdered mother and father nearby.

I marveled at the beauty of the ethnic blanket. I shuddered that the child could not feel its warmth in this horrendous setting.

Six months later a special edition of *Life* arrived containing the best photography of the year. Among them, little Valmir and her blanket. The photo was taken by Adam Brown, a Canadian journalist, near the village of Obrinje.

You might recall another picture that made the papers last fall. It was of an ethnic Albanian woman feeding a bottle to a six-week-old baby, said to be the only survivor of a massacre near Obrinje. The baby was wrapped in a beautifully embroidered blanket, looking safe and content. But the woman's face mirrored the horror. The baby's name was Diturie Deliaj. We must assume it was this baby's family murdered in the woods.

It's spring, and we crave the return of warm sun, the trees and shrubs coming to life after a long winter.

Valmir will never come to life, never feel the sun. Who knows what has happened to Diturie? How do we look at these children, turn the page, and say, "Who cares?"

Compassion is the bottom line of existence, for all of us. If we don't have it, we become as inhuman as those who are mowing down women and children.

The flowers on that blanket in the woods near Obrinje are what I think of this Easter Sunday. They do not find themselves on a perky Easter bonnet. They are not crocuses or daffodils peeking from the warming earth to represent a new beginning. They represent a proud culture. They are on a blanket covering a murdered child.

SUITING UP FOR A SWIM

April 2000

It's here. That dreaded time we must face up to every spring: Trying on a bathing suit. Screeching sounds from dressing rooms are being heard everywhere.

When you are fortunate enough to get an early vacation in a warm climate, the chore comes earlier than usual. And it is a chore. There have been years when I could put off the ultimate chagrin until June or July.

I am planning to visit my son in Florida this month, which meant seeking a suit in February or March.

So I've been through it. It's not pretty.

Now it's your turn.

The first glance in the dressing-room mirror is comparable to chewing aspirin. It leaves a bad taste in your mouth. You might even weep.

I am not eighteen or twenty-five or thirty-five. It has been downhill since, well, I'm not sure. I just know it's getting worse. I admit my age; I just don't admit my body shape.

Most stores have a no-return policy on swimsuits, but it would be nice if you could do the trying-on at home. There, you could view yourself by candlelight or a dim 25-watt bulb, which might take some of the emphasis off the reality in the mirror. A glass or two of wine might help. You could shriek into a pillow or throw something at the dog, just to take the edge off the experience. That's an advantage. Release hostility.

The reality is that time changes everything, which sounds much like a lyric from one of Andrew Lloyd Webber's musicals. But I'm not singing. What a downer this is, buying a swimsuit.

I don't pretend to buy a new one every year, and especially the past ten years I have tried not to, simply to save myself the depression that ultimately follows. I wear them until they have lost enough stretch to follow my true curves. Not a pretty sight.

Is it an ego thing? You betcha. It's all about remembering a tight, taut, lithe, and firm body which, you assumed, would never change.

Weight is one thing, but skin changes. I think the first time you are brushing your hair and notice flabby upper arms in the mirror, you know the process has begun. You just don't face it.

"Hey, what's wrong with this mirror?" is a likely refrain.

I know women my age and beyond who remain slim and have flat tummies, but there's no denying the skin covering our bones begins to hang a bit, and then more than a bit, and that crepe-paper-like rippled effect announces you are aging.

A rubdown with Crisco oil wouldn't hurt.

Trips to the gym as a remedy? Maybe. But it means constant attention, and who has time for that? The clock is ticking even as you climb your stairs, sip your diet drink, or do your pushups.

I am firmly reminded at swimsuit time, time is not on my side.

A guttural "good grief" escaped my throat when I tried on suits a few weeks ago. As my knees are exposed for the first time after a covered-up winter, I think, "Venetian blind. My knees look like a Venetian blind." Instinctively I reach down to pull the skin tight, as it once was. I forget when, but it was. It never used to be wrinkled like that. Or did it?

If you are wearing knee-highs or trouser socks as you pose in your suit with the "moderate cut" legs, you wonder, "If these are moderate cut, what must high cut be? Under your arms?" Well, of course, you know you have looked like this essentially the past thirty years.

Being called a "senior" has its advantages. But it's hard not to fret when we are constantly being reminded of our aging.

They're talking on the six o'clock news about an "elderly" woman being robbed. She's two years younger than I am! High school buddies are observing golden wedding anniversaries.

Every day, a reminder of time fleeting, but never moreso than in the dressing room with a swimsuit.

I vowed I would never wear a bathing suit with a skirt. They were designed for older women, to conceal imperfect figures. We all know that.

Forget that's who I am at present. I still won't wear one. No, I am seeking a suit with far more coverage, maybe long sleeves. Maybe bloomers, maybe a turtleneck. A skimpy skirt won't do it.

My ankles are still in pretty good shape, as are my earlobes. I expect to get glances at the beach. You're thinking it would be the bloomers. I'd prefer to think it's my ankles. Forever young. Va-va-va-voom.

TEA AND CRUMPETS

July 2001

I have rediscovered crumpets because Ruggeri's, the small market in my neighborhood, is carrying packages of Farm Country crumpets, made in the States and fat free. Smashing.

A crumpet, by the way, is similar to an English muffin, but flatter. You don't slice a crumpet.

The consistency of the dough is also different. As I am trying to find words to describe them, my mouth is watering, and I want to race home and have one—or two or three—immediately.

I will hold off my longings in order to tell you about a crumpet, if you don't already know.

Hailing from the British Isles, they are small yeast-raised breads of unsweetened batter that is poured into special rings, then baked on a stovetop. So says *A Food Lover's Companion* by Evan Jones (Harper & Row).

The commercials for English muffins with their "nooks and crannies" would fit crumpets as well, but the description of their texture and appearance goes like this: They are "wrinkled and full of crumples." Like an English muffin, one side is smooth, the other full of tiny holes.

Nooks and crannies is probably more appetizing than full of crumples, which in Webster's as a noun is equivalent to a crease or wrinkle.

A crumpet is best toasted. It is very white in the package, so tanning it somewhat gives it a much more appealing look.

In many ways, a crumpet looks very much like a small pancake when the batter first hits the grill. It's about the size of a hockey puck.

You know how those little bubbles pop in the batter as a pancake cooks? That's what a crumpet looks like before toasting.

What do you put on a crumpet? Anything your little heart desires, as far as I can tell. I suppose you can eat them any time of day, but history relates to them as tea cakes, so I assume teatime, as in British tradition, is best.

I eat them for breakfast, lunch, or dinner, by jove, without tea. I have no couth.

I assume they would be great with peanut butter and maybe even as a pizza base, or part of an eggs Benedict concoction. I just know they are good. They are chewy, by the way, moreso than a muffin.

They've even been described as "rather rubbery" in consistency. Chewy is a nicer word.

Some years ago, living in New York, I met Marylou, who lived in Canada but always spoke with a kind of British accent.

Marylou had different tastes, which made knowing her interesting. We were pals with Blanche, who was Hawaiian, my second acquaintance from another culture, who also had different tastes. She used to keep yogurt on her windowsill (in winter) at the Barbizon Hotel where we lived while pursuing our careers in the Big Apple.

She also loved poi. I found both yogurt and poi utterly disgusting.

But Marylou fascinated me because everywhere we went, she asked for crumpets. I was learning so much beyond my small world of grilled cheese sandwiches.

We never found a crumpet. Of course, we were eating in hamburger joints or from street-vendor carts most of the time.

In later years, when our Manhattan adventure was over and we went back to our respective hometowns, Marylou tootled down from Toronto to visit me. That was her word for traveling.

She brought crumpets. She arrived in a snowstorm driving what looked like a toy car with plastic windows. We sat in the kitchen and had tea and crumpets as the storm raged.

And that was the first and last time I had a crumpet, until this recent discovery.

The other thing Marylou always asked for as a drink was a Pimm's Cup. It was embarrassing when we went to a neighborhood restaurant in a shot-and-a-beer town and she asked, "I say, do you have Pimm's Cup?"

This was a restaurant where waitresses wore big buttons on their aprons that asked, "Do yunz want wine?"

So, no, they didn't have Pimm's Cup.

Now, you won't have the same memories as you bite into a crumpet, but I was remembering my friends from other places as I plunked my second crumpet into the toaster the other day.

Jolly good. I'm hooked.

And for a bit of trivia, it seems crumpet also has a vulgar meaning (depending on where you're from), as in "a bit of crumpet," meaning a sexually available woman.

I thought that was a strumpet.

At any rate, if you are going to England, be careful what you ask for.

GRILLED CHEESE IS A TURN-ON

November 2001

I've been teased most of my adult life about liking grilled cheese sandwiches. I've preferred them since I was young and liked little else. Certainly not veggies.

It probably hit its peak when friends and I went to lunch at Kaufmann's tea room during the week of a store promotion of France some years ago. That included French cuisine on the lunch and dinner menus. They were extensive and impressive. We read the offerings aloud because saying *patisserie* or *avec vin blanc* made the choices seem all the more delectable.

It took time to read the menu and even more time forming the French descriptions on our tongues, but finally everyone made a selection and grinned with anticipation as to what would appear.

Me? "Could I have a grilled cheese?" I did not ask in French. I got Gruyère (I think) on French bread, of course. They have never let me forget that. It wasn't the first time, nor would it be the last. When in doubt, ask if they have grilled cheese. And I am often in doubt when it comes to ordering in a restaurant. Long menus confuse me.

So, it was with great delight I read an article about artist Jeff Koons that appeared in the *New York Times Magazine* last summer. In the article, Koons expresses his soft spot for this "humble American sandwich."

Koons is described in the article as he is today: "part pop, part surreal, part deadpan, part wild." The writer asks us to pretend Andy Warhol and Salvador Dali had a son together.

That boy would be Koons in a nutshell.

Koons and I obviously have nothing in common except for this grilled cheese sandwich thing. As an artist, Koons is said to "run rings around the psychoanalytic establishment when it comes to sexual interpretations of ordinary things." And he has done artworks depicting my favorite sandwich. I won't let my mind go there.

While Koons's reputation is that he pushes buttons, a recent development seems to be his art getting to his stomach. He actually picked up the history of the grilled cheese sandwich on the Internet and then invited the New York writer of the online story to dinner and to shop for the ingredients. He bought Velveeta slices, Kraft singles, Kraft Natural Cheddar, D'Agostino's Medium Cheddar, Wonder Bread, Thomas's English muffins, Martin's Dutch taste potato bread, and Land O'Lakes butter.

This surely sounded like a binge by an addict, much more addicted than I. But I was fascinated because what he did was make a variety of sandwiches, combining cheeses and buttering the bread differently each time before he dumped it into a skillet. He also used a sandwich-maker for one version.

Koons's memories of his mother fixing him such sandwiches when he came home from high school and, later, when he made them himself in college, seem to have triggered this obsession.

In that we share a memory. Grilled cheese sandwiches and chicken noodle soup was often our Sunday supper when I was growing up. It was one of my favorites.

When I began to putter in the kitchen and my mother would allow me to do certain things by myself, a grilled cheese was easy. To be honest, I never got much further than that when it came to cooking prowess. But I made a mean (and evenly toasted) sandwich.

As a teenager, I found date night often meant going to a certain restaurant after a movie or football game. I always ordered two grilled cheese sandwiches with mayonnaise and pickles. I can smell them as I write. They didn't get much better than that.

Cholesterol? Who knew? I was, in fact, skinny. And I ate both of them.

Koons, however, gets a bit more poetic about the concoction. He is quoted as saying, "Grilled cheese is like an aphrodisiac, and it makes you think of being on the beach and getting a lot of sun. You get vitamin D, and you get kind of sexualized."

Whazatt?

Hmmmm. I love the beach but have never dreamed of a grilled cheese sandwich while soaking up the sun. Each has its place. One is sustenance. One is soul-redeeming.

"When you are cooking that bread," Koons goes on to say, "you're giving it a tan, and it's getting sexually excited."

Well, I'll be. Melted cheese on burnt bread can do that? I'm going to keep my eye on the next sandwich I flip in the skillet.

Who needs adult films when you can watch cheese sizzle?

I never knew.

TRASH AND TREASURE

March 2002

Me, in the same category as Andy Warhol? Be careful what you wish for. I am not sure when collecting becomes an obsession, or when junk becomes stuff, and stuff becomes memorabilia, and you become a millionaire.

The truth is, when I read about "Possession Obsession: Objects from Andy Warhol's Personal Collection," now on view at the North Side museum, I felt connected.

I, too, have lots of stuff. I took stock of my cupboards, desk drawers, and shelves filled with treasured tchotchkes and couldn't decide whether it was time to clean house or call the auction house.

For one shining moment, I was deterred from filling trash bags with my loot. I dreamed of an auction with chic people begging to own my...what? My hangers, my pencils, my dry-cleaning bags, or dying houseplants?

Well, I'm already laughing just imagining the value of a stash of Cool Whip plastic containers. I have a lot of those. I don't have large quantities of everything, but I do seem to hoard paper clips, pencils, and rubber bands—and those Cool Whip containers, for leftovers.

Like Andy; like I told you.

You know those packets printed with "Extra Buttons" that you receive with new clothing? I probably have every packet of buttons I ever clipped from a sweater, dress, or jacket over the past fifty years. Excluding the buttons, much of my stuff is saved because of sentiment—curls cut from my head in 1934, for instance.

I have scrapbooks and boxes of pictures of people whose

names I can't even remember, including New Guinea natives in the nude. No, I don't keep them for thrills. Andy might have. My father kept these and many other pictures from his World War II duty in New Guinea. Now I have them.

I have kept all the sympathy cards received when my mother, father, and sister passed away. Priceless is the value of those cards at the times they were sent. But why do I keep them twenty-five years later?

Why do I keep albums from the 1940s I never play or my son's broken childhood crayons? They collect dust, they take up space, these things, this stuff. What about fifty years of newspaper clippings of my work, yellowed with age and crackling to the touch? Or baby announcements from friends whose babies must now have children and grandchildren of their own? Great grandchildren would not be out of the question. Why do we keep these things?

I'm not sure how all of this begins. I certainly don't know if Andy knew what his treasures would bring in dollars and cents or if he was so darned smart, he saw the potential in what he was gathering. Or, if he simply had fun. Maybe Fiesta Ware made him smile.

When I'm gone, will my Spiro Agnew watch bring anything but giggles? Andy had a Fred Flintstone watch in his Sotheby's 1988 auction. As an artist, I suppose he saw what most of us don't see in certain ordinary items.

I always remembered the magazine article "Long Live Andy" by Glenn O'Brien, which began, "Andy Warhol's death was his best publicity stunt."

Maybe you have to leave this world in order to give meaning to possessions. I'd rather not do that.

Andy's life was devoted to extending the envelope of overkill, wrote O'Brien, who had worked for Warhol at *Interview* magazine. Andy knew that too much was never enough. He was sometimes called "the mad hoarder."

Me, too. Too many pencils and paper clips and buttons, plastic dry-cleaning bags, and hangers fill nooks and crannies. I did not recognize my obsessive ways until Andy made it so cool.

Andy would be laughing at our insatiable appetite for all that he touched.

Lint from his dryer screen would probably have chic people bidding furiously. What about my lint? Not likely. But I am obsessive. Witness, the piles of pantyhose still packaged, bought and never worn; hotel guest shampoos, which I can't resist taking and never use; and used kitchen sponges I might need for a dirty job some day, with all that bacteria. And every straw basket that ever came to me with fruit or flowers is in my basement.

There's more: piles of magazines no longer published and beige sweaters. I hate to tell you how many have space in my house.

What do I have the most of? Lipsticks and seashells.

I also have silent film star Ramon Navarro's autograph and a leather E.T. doll in my "possession."

Why I have them, or my blond baby curls, is anybody's guess. I doubt they have value to anyone but me. Still, I think it's time to haul to the curb at least some of the stuff. I'll keep the curls and the watch, some of the lipsticks, photographs, E.T., pantyhose, a few hangers, plastic bags, and Cool Whip containers...see, I'm obsessively possessive, just like Andy. Who knew?

Parting is such sweet sorrow. So is parting with stuff, it would seem.

FANTASTIC PLASTIC
FLAMINGO

June 2002

A friend called the other day just to see what I was up to. I anchored the phone on my shoulder as I continued to perform the chore I was doing and answer her question at the same time.

"I'm washing my pink flamingo," I replied to her inquiry.

Well, she asked, didn't it wash itself? There was silence. Of course there would be. And then, she said, quite awkwardly, "Uhhhhh, I didn't know you had a flamingo."

My flamingo is, of course, not the real thing. But I was scrubbing the winter's grime from the somewhat faded pink body and when she asked what I was doing, I answered without thinking.

It is a whimsical yard ornament I ordered from a catalog a couple of years ago. I love it. I have since learned it has a name: the "Bouncin' Head" lawn flamingo. It has a body and head of wood, and the two are joined by a long narrow sheet of metal that allows the head to bob in a breeze. Its promotional literature says, "Given a gentle tap, he'll pretty much agree to anything." Its legs are two narrow metal rods inserted into the bottom of the wooden belly. It is much maligned, this creature, though fans of the PPF (pink plastic flamingo) refer to it as "splendor on the grass."

The pink flamingo has a position of respect in Florida, where it decorates everything from tableware to sheets, beach towels, and flip-flops. Here, however, the plastic flamingo has always been considered tacky. Why is that? If you see one in someone's yard, you kind of titter and assume someone is playing a joke. On the other hand, you can almost tell when someone has placed a flamingo or two in a garden with a feeling of love and respect.

They are oblivious to ridicule, as they should be. They refuse to concede the pink flamingo is a laughing matter.

I have to admit I never wanted one of the plastic ones, even though they have been gracing (or disturbing) America's lawns for more than forty years in either the feeding or standing pose. And when I saw the real bird in a zoo setting in New Jersey, I thought it was plastic. The real thing looks every inch like the sculpted plastic version. They are rather unusual-looking, that's for sure, but I don't know how they became the butt of jokes. Isn't a plastic deer, sheep, or duck just as silly?

I had a new respect for the birds after seeing them live and taking off in a flock at a California preserve. Did you ever see one fly? Such grace and beauty.

You can get a flamingo wind wheel, jumbo wire picks, bird feeder, trellis, flag, all-weather statue, welcome hanger, or wind chimes if you log on to FlamingoMania.com. You can also get a "Flamingo Road" sign. There was once a tacky TV series by that name. You see? Guilt by association. Not the bird's fault.

Don Featherstone is the father of the pink plastic flamingo concept. He invented it when he first went to work for Union Products in Leominster, Massachusetts, in 1957, right out of art school. He sculpted it out of clay, and that was used to make a plaster cast, and the cast was used for aluminum dies to mold the plastic.

He stayed at Union, buying the firm from the former owners in 1996. He retired last year. They manufacture between 600 and 800 products, and Featherstone sculpted all of the originals, including ducks, penguins, and gnome lawn ornaments.

"In the summer," Featherstone said in a 1997 interview, "I keep fifty-seven flamingos in my own yard, but in the winter I have two white ones called Snomingos, and seventeen penguins."

In early America, there was no lawn ornamentation. When Europeans started bringing over bronze statuary, few people could afford them. Before plastics, only rich people could afford to have poor taste, says Featherstone, who obviously has a sense of humor. His own neighbors used to hate his flamingos and complained all the time. But when they moved to Florida, they asked him to send them some.

This is his theory: He did something people enjoyed, something amusing, when he created the pink plastic flamingo, and that's more satisfying than designing something destructive, like the atom bomb. People who put out flamingos, he says, are friendlier than most people. Well, mine isn't the PPF, but close. It makes me a nicer person.

DARE TO BELIEVE

December 2002

My thoughts at Christmas:

- I rely on what is old. It always seems new.
- I can't be cynical. I can't be a disbeliever.
- I don't care what they call the shopping season. I embrace it.
- I know why we celebrate Christmas. It isn't in an ad or a slogan. It's in my heart.
- I make no apologies for loving the season.
- I have heard reindeer on the roof.
- I aspire to having the perfect tree and sometimes succeed. It has, at times, fallen over. Such is life.
- I love the hustle and bustle and mistletoe, festive shopping bags, and creative store windows.
- Family and friends: They are gifts we will never exchange for another size.
- Reasons to smile: Surprises, candles, a dog wearing a red ribbon, a child's eyes of wonder.
- I love being home for the holidays.
- I was born to love the holidays, and I do.

So, sue me.

Most of what I feel comes from the era in which I was raised. It comes from days when being told Santa Claus was real was not looked upon as psychologically damaging. So, we believed. I feel no worse for that parental "abuse." I believed until I was eleven and tried to hang on at twelve, but I had grown too wise. I regret that wisdom.

I don't think it messed me up for life. It could have made me too trusting, and naive, but since when is that a bad thing?

Daring to believe makes all things possible.

As I grew to learn that my parents had a distinct hand in making dreams come true Christmas morning, I was none the worse for knowing. I knew they loved me. What else mattered?

I had felt the magic. That magic, seen now through keener eyes, not to mention the knowledge that reindeer can't fly, was worth the deception—a hundred times over. They showed me magic. It was the gift of a lifetime.

The perfect tree; Mother in her apron; Daddy called out to deliver a Christmas Eve baby; my sister twisting bows into art on packages; the warmth of our modest home and the smells—ah, the smells of Christmas.

This is not to suggest that being upfront with your youngsters about jolly ol' St. Nick isn't fine and dandy, if that is the choice you make.

We—and I refer to the adult world celebrating Christmas or not—have already shortened the years of childhood by forcing our children to grow up too fast—whiz kids by their terrible twos. There's no time for innocence or naiveté.

My generation hung onto childhood, basic and simple, as long as we could. I took full advantage. I imagined, I dreamed, I played, and longer than most. The presents, the sparkle, and—if prayers were answered—a snowfall made the holiday even more joyful.

Of course, I wrote to Santa. My wish list always seemed to include a doll, a game, and oranges. I have never understood why I always asked for oranges.

Nostalgia is an integral part of Christmas. It doesn't matter what name the retailers choose for the shopping season. I think about the joy. I struggle more and more to be that child again at this time of year. Antagonists fight me. They seem determined to stifle the joy.

NO HANKY NO PANKY

October 2006

A rainy day brings mixed blessings.

You might decide to clean your closets and dresser drawers to dismiss the dripping rain off the porch roof, the moist screens in the windows, the dampness in the air.

It sometimes brings us in touch with the past.

So, on a recent rainy day, I tackled my dresser drawers and closets, seeking giveaways.

As I reached into pockets of certain items of clothing that had been hanging for months, I found some forgotten handkerchiefs. In the drawers I found a few more, folded neatly in a satin "handkerchief box."

Remember them? Do they make those any longer? Mine has a matching quilted satin glove box, which now contains two or three beaded necklaces.

Gloves, the short white ones, bit the dust long ago. I suppose handkerchiefs, especially lovely lacy ones with an embroidered initial or sprig of lily-of-the-valley, are a thing of the past.

Kleenex will do. You toss it after use. I'm not sure if men still carry those large, white, folded handkerchiefs. A few men will tuck pocket squares in their jackets to be stylish. Not the same thing. Too small for serious use.

I did note when watching a rerun of the 1998 movie *You've Got Mail*, Tom Hanks took out his handkerchief to wipe Meg Ryan's tears. How real is that these days?

So, handkerchiefs are on my mind this particular day. I even decided to wash all of them, and iron them when they were still slightly damp, as my mother used to do. No giveaways. They're lovely, I thought.

As I was pressing them, I was reminded of Albert, known to my family as "the linen man." On a regular basis Albert would come knocking on our door back in the '30s and '40s. He was the true traveling salesman. He always looked tired and worn, as I am sure he was. It wasn't easy traveling with your goods to make a living. My father always bought something as a surprise for my mother, but he made Albert work hard for the sale. He did, however, leave smiling, as I recall.

In his suitcase, amid the dinner tablecloths, dresser scarves, and doilies were handkerchiefs—beautiful ones, embroidered and edged with lace, mostly all of them white, sometimes with contrasting embroidery.

Albert's gift to my sister and me at the end of each visit would be one of these handkerchiefs. We weren't as appreciative as we should have been, being so young, but we were encouraged by our mother to say thank you...and then we raced out to play.

When we visited large department stores, my mother always stopped and looked at the case displays of handkerchiefs, and very often she made a purchase, together with a pair of gloves. You could never have too many handkerchiefs or gloves.

Sending a dainty handkerchief in a greeting card for Christmas or a birthday was a way to let someone know you cared. With an initial, even more special.

Through the years when I visited New York, I often stopped at the linen stores in Times Square, and usually came away with a handkerchief or two.

I always thought of Albert.

A handkerchief is so ladylike. It's so lovely. It triggers such a warm feeling.

My parents, Milton Harlan and Elizabeth Cloud. He was a physician in Uniontown for fifty years and she was a housewife and mother. Below, with one of our pets, Mitzi.

We were introduced to Stone Harbor, New Jersey, where photo above left was taken, by my mother's sister, Edna, in 1947. My son and I would also spend many summer vacations there. On the right, my father in a photo taken while stationed in New Guinea during World War II.

1955

1950

1958

Just before going underground in a gold mine in Canada (my first by-line story), above left, and at age nineteen, above right, playing a sophisticated older woman in a play at Jennerstown Mountain Playhouse. And more glamor, above, in Bernardine *at the Pittsburgh Playhouse.*

1952

1951

1966

At my desk, top, at the Evening
Standard, *where I became a society
editor for five years. Above left, my
publicity shot as a hopeful actress in
New York, and in a favorite title role in*
Auntie Mame *at Little Lake Theater.*

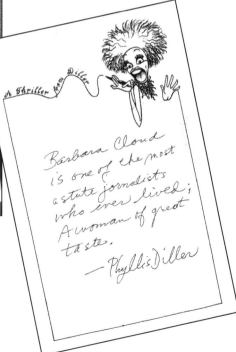

Barbara Cloud
is one of the most
astute journalists
who ever lived;
A woman of great
taste.

— Phyllis Diller

When Pittsburgh Models Club honored Phyllis Diller in 1966, I presented her with the unusual award. I first interviewed her in the 1960s and she only got better with age. My last story was on the occasion of her ninetieth birthday.

127

1968

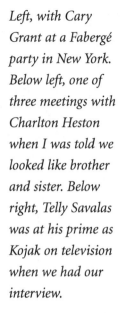

Left, with Cary Grant at a Fabergé party in New York. Below left, one of three meetings with Charlton Heston when I was told we looked like brother and sister. Below right, Telly Savalas was at his prime as Kojak on television when we had our interview.

1974

128

1966

I saw my resemblance to Sophie Tucker, above right, known as the "red hot mama" when we met at the Variety Club. Joan Crawford's sadness struck me during this interview, above. She sent me the thank-you note before her daughter Christina's devastating Mommie Dearest *book was published. The actress knew it was being written but died in 1977 before its release.*

JOAN CRAWFORD

February 8, 1959

Dear Barbara,

It was such a joy to meet you while we were in Pittsburgh, and thank you so much for your charming article about us. I want to thank you especially, Barbara, for quoting me accurately about Christina. I am so deeply grateful to you for your kindliness in your writing, and for your graciousness.

All good wishes to you, and I am looking forward to seeing you again to thank you personally.

Joan Crawford

129

1959

1978

1961

Troy Donahue (A Summer Place) *was an up-and-coming young actor, top photo, and Katharine Cornell, above right, was an established star when we met. Meeting Myrtle Brady, above left, remains as inspirational to me as meeting a movie star.*

Bill Blass, left, at the opening of Saks Fifth Avenue in Pittsburgh. Below, taking notes in a Seventh Avenue showroom as model on the right shows latest designer collection. When designer Ralph Lauren learned my birthday (October 16) was two days after his, he sent a note with flowers. He often sent notes to editors after reading reviews of his collections.

1977

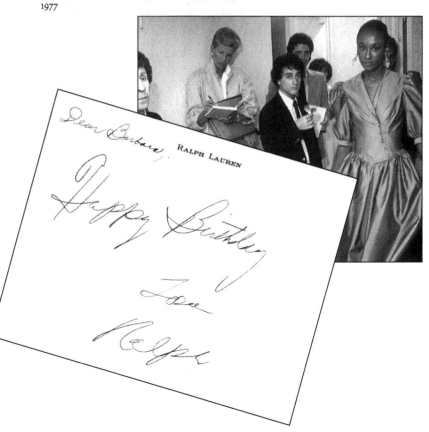

Dear Barbara,

RALPH LAUREN

Happy Birthday

Love

Ralph

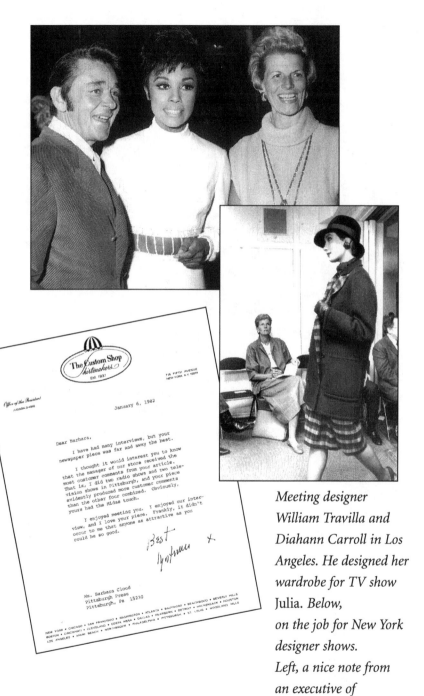

The Custom Shop
Shirtmakers
Est. 1937

718 FIFTH AVENUE
NEW YORK, N.Y. 10019

Office of the President
AVENON 2-4266

January 6, 1982

Dear Barbara,

I have had many interviews, but your newspaper piece was far and away the best.

I thought it would interest you to know that the manager of our store received the most customer comments from your article. That is, I did two radio shows and two television shows in Pittsburgh, and your piece evidently produced more customer comments than the other four combined. Obviously, yours had the Midas touch.

I enjoyed meeting you. I enjoyed our interview, and I love your piece. Frankly, it didn't occur to me that anyone as attractive as you could be so good.

Best
[signature]

Ms. Barbara Cloud
Pittsburgh Press
Pittsburgh, Pa 15230

NEW YORK • CHICAGO • SAN FRANCISCO • WASHINGTON • ATLANTA • BALTIMORE • BEACHWOOD • BEVERLY HILLS
BOSTON • CINCINNATI • CLEVELAND • COSTA MESA • DALLAS • DEARBORN • DETROIT • HACKENSACK • HOUSTON
LOS ANGELES • MIAMI BEACH • NORTHBROOK • PHILADELPHIA • PITTSBURGH • ST. LOUIS • WOODLAND HILLS

*Meeting designer
William Travilla and
Diahann Carroll in Los
Angeles. He designed her
wardrobe for TV show
Julia. Below,
on the job for New York
designer shows.
Left, a nice note from
an executive of
The Custom Shop.*

1978

2000

And may 2002 bring you healthy, carefree days with lots to laugh about. Your column continues to be one of my week's highlights —
Cordelia May

Above, getting a story firsthand as a model for a Symphony Gala, and on the left, holding my Golden Aldo *with Men's Fashion Association Director Chip Tolbert. Bottom left, my "prom date" with Marvin Hamlisch.*

1991

1971

Surprised by lifetime achievement award in 1991.
Former Pittsburgher Tom Julian, MFA assistant
fashion director, is at left. Just a few days before my
son, Drew, was born in 1971, I was presented with a
fashion writer's award (FRANY) in New York by
designer Vincent Monte-Sano.

Sharing a laugh with Eileen Ford of the Ford Model Agency, above, during a visit to Pittsburgh. Among many notes saved through the years, this one, right, from Estee Lauder showed why she succeeded in the cosmetic industry. She was always appreciative of the press.

From the desk of Estée Lauder

July, 1980

Dear Miss Cloud,

Thank you for sending a copy of your story. I enjoyed every word of it--almost as much as our meeting! The occasion was a pleasure for me and I couldn't be happier with your editorial. I thought it expressed the spirit of my company perfectly.

Sharing information on the latest developments in beauty products with your readers offers them a welcome service, and I am certain they were happy to have a look "behind the scenes".

Your coverage is important to me and your interest in news of my company is so appreciated.

Warmest thoughts,

[signed] Fondly, Estée Lauder

Miss Barbara Cloud
Fashion Editor
Pittsburgh Press
34 Boulevard of the Allies
Pittsburgh, Pennsylvania 15230

135

It wasn't all glamour. Assignments included fishing, catching and cooking fresh trout, left, and learning tricks of the grooming trade for my cocker spaniel, Soot, below. I also "interviewed" Rajah, below left, who was retiring from touring with the circus at age twenty-six. Variety kept me on my toes.

1963

1964

1981

Instilling youngsters with desire to keep Pittsburgh streets free of litter inspired many columns over the years. This was in Market Square. Imagine my surprise, left, when my editor asked me to go to Allegheny Wharf and get some fishing tips from young anglers.

1960

My only sister, B.J., who passed away in 1998, was a society editor in Uniontown while I was in college, and I never thought I would follow in her footsteps. B.J., below at Fallingwater.

The subject of many columns since he was born in 1971, my son, Drew, married Margaret Marie Garcia in an all-white wedding on the beach at Cabo San Lucas, April 7, 2007. It was magical.

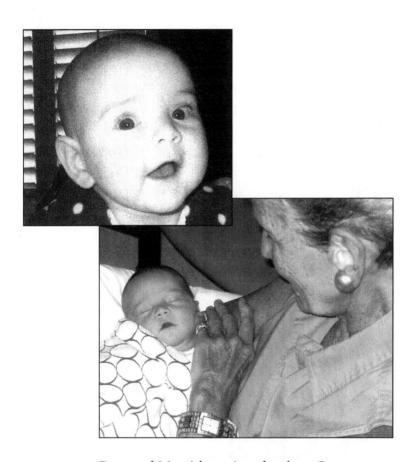

Drew and Maggie's precious daughter, Grace Elizabeth Marie, at six months, above. A proud and grateful Nana, below, with Gracie recovering from pneumonia in Arizona hospital. She was just two days old.

A happy and healthy Grace, eight months, and her Nana, a bit older, at a Phoenix Suns NBA game in December 2008. Below, the Cloud family at Grace's baptism. I can only wish her love all her life. She's the reason for this book.

2008

"I helped establish the Nina Hyde Center for Breast Cancer Research at Georgetown University because she was a good writer and I knew how hard she fought before she died in 1990. I was battling a brain tumor at the same time."

—Ralph Lauren, 1994

"I was staff caricaturist for the LA Times some years ago, but caricatures are something you cannot study. I enjoy drawing because it is great relaxation."

—Xavier Cugat, 1960

"I'd like to see other people go through what actors often do and be as brave. Pittsburgh audiences are tough. I'm not sure I want to face them soon again."

—Howard Keel, 1963

"Maybe I'm not selling any records, but I'm selling two hundred plates of spaghetti a day in my restaurant in Florida."

—Julius LaRosa, 1960

"It's ironic but as kids we used to pick favorite animals and mine was the gorilla. I used to want to be a stunt man or a pilot, but if I was embarrassed to tell people what I do now for a living, I wouldn't be doing it."

—Bob Woolf, NBA Phoenix Suns Gorilla Mascot, 2006

the white house

the runway

over the rainbow

broadway

pittsburgh

new york

madison avenue

new york

carnegie museum

madison avenue

los angeles

paris stone harbor

the runw

florence

mexico

home california pittsburg

dusseldorf

the stage

Where

OVER THE RAINBOW

October 20, 1961

How do you explain Judy Garland?

It is altogether possible that if she just walked around a stage and waved her arms and blew kisses to the audience she would have a following second to none.

She creates the magic which is what entertainment is all about and yet you cannot pinpoint just exactly where it is that she manages to pull you in from the audience as a bee to honey, as puppets in her hand and she controls the strings.

At the Civic auditorium last night when she presented the concert that had Carnegie Hall and the Hollywood Bowl both bursting at the seams, she scored another triumph if attendance is any criterion.

There were 12,219 ticket holders who witnessed Miss Garland's performance. Many were fans, many were curious, many attended with a "show me" attitude. What is it, Miss Garland, which makes sentimentalists of us all, makes us burst into applause when you simply move a finger, leave the stage for a drink of water, or stop in the middle of a number to adjust some of the technical equipment?

But then, why question it? It is there and it was obvious last night that the audience was in love with the singer who cavorted on stage, backed up, to be sure, by an impressive musical aggregation and Mort Lindsey, her conductor.

Miss Garland does cavort, you see. It isn't simply a matter of singing a song, which she does like no one else I can think of. If everyone has as much fun watching her perform as she seems to have while doing it, then it is indeed a perfect balance of entertainment, a love match without a quarrel.

Maybe that in itself is the secret. She appears to love what she is doing but if this is not true, then she deserves to be known as a great actress in addition to a great singer.

The tremor in her voice that would make you recognize Judy Garland without sight is still there, just as it was when she performed her magic tricks in a dozen or more films, *The Wizard of Oz* being particularly notable.

She was young Dorothy of that film most of the evening. She was youthful and she made the audience feel the same way. You could hear the familiar laugh when she came close to the microphone, the shy laugh of Andy Hardy's girlfriend, and she wasn't even trying.

Is she fat? Who cares. Certainly she couldn't have looked more chic than she did in the black street-length dress and red satin jacket studded with sparkling stones which caught the light from the spots and danced all over the stage.

And the second half of the show found Miss Garland wearing black silk slacks and a multicolored jacket of iridescents.

She moved about the stage in such a way that you felt the gaiety of the song she was presenting. And the same feeling came when she took her stance in front of the microphone, feet spread apart as if to hold onto some gravity as she reached for, and found, that last note which would bring down the house.

Vitality…it might be that. Choice of songs, such as the familiar "Bells Are Ringing," "Stormy Weather," "The Man That Got Away," "San Francisco," "Come Rain or Come Shine"… it could be this that brings over 12,000 people to a performance.

The crowd applauded if they had the faintest hint from the musical introduction as to the song she was going to sing. Many of those attending called to her by name… "We can't hear you,

Judy"… "Turn the lights on, Judy, we want to see you."

And there is the whole story of Judy Garland. She has to be seen to be believed. The audience wanted her to be "in touch" with the star last night and that was the pity of it. Some could not hear as well as they wanted to and the stillness of the auditorium proved they were giving her their full attention.

She sang "Over the Rainbow" as her last number…supposedly. But the audience stood up and cheered and screamed for more and Miss Garland shook hands with a few of the people sitting close to the stage. This brought even more applause and more hands reaching out to shake hers.

She came back six times, four of those times she simply walked around the stage like a child and threw kisses to the audience, most of them already standing with coats in hand, realizing the show was over but reluctant to leave for fear of missing something.

She did sing two more numbers, "Swanee" and "Chicago," and they did turn on the lights, which probably brought more applause than any song she sang all evening.

Now they could see her. Now they could believe her.

MISS ANN AND THE WESTINGHOUSE BOYS

June 1963

She's not a very big woman. The place where she works is as unglamorous as you can imagine. She is not an heiress and she does not have the measurements of a beauty queen, and yet forty or fifty men openly express admiration for her.

She's Mrs. Ann McShane, the kindest wash lady in the world. If you don't believe it, ask the graduating seniors and athletes at Westinghouse High School. Mrs. McShane has been a cleaning woman at the school for twenty years. Three years ago she was asked to take charge of the laundry and she said she'd try it for one week.

She retired this week and the future athletes at the school who have never known her smiling Irish face are the losers.

Those who have come in contact with her the past few years have only love and respect for the gentle woman with the slight brogue who arrived in this country from County Antrim, Ireland, in 1921.

Miss Ann, the affectionate name bestowed by "her boys," took time out from her last day of school (and washing) to talk about the new friends she has made. During the conversation many of the senior boys who have laughed and joked with her during football seasons poked their heads in the door of the laundry room to say goodbye. They deposited large photos with endearing messages, boxes of cookies, and other small mementoes for Miss Ann. One boy saved seventy-five cents so that he could have a party for her.

She wears a watch, which was a gift when the team won one of its many championships. A necklace with a single pearl pendant was presented to her last Christmas.

"I'm so proud of these," she said quietly. "I'll miss my boys. I'll have to take time later to read all the verses they've written on pictures and cards. They are beautiful sentiments."

Dr. Paul Felton, principal, has known Miss Ann for many years. "It's quite unique these days," he said. "She is a woman who loves her work. She has taken what many consider a menial chore and she made a profession of it. You can't ask for a higher accolade than that."

Football coach Pete Dimperio can't find enough complimentary adjectives for Miss Ann. "She's really something. She has time for everyone."

Through all of the praise, Miss Ann sat quietly, often excusing herself to hand out some towels or accept a token from one of the students. The job often meant laundering some eight hundred towels per day, plus uniforms.

Recalling a memorable day at the school, she snickered a bit and then told of the time she promised the team a treat of ice cream if they won the game. She was so sure they would win, she ordered the ice cream, but it was a sad day. The boys passed her laundry room crying like babies.

"I cried, too," she said, "and someone wondered if it was because my job was too hard for me. I told them no, I was crying because my boys lost the game."

"It's difficult to describe what she has done for the boys here. She's as near irreplaceable as anyone can be," said Dr. Felton.

"Every year the athletes name the person who has contributed most to victory," explained Mr. Dimperio. "I used to win," he smiled. "For the past two years it has been Miss Ann."

EN ROUTE TO DUSSELDORF

February 1995

I noted the long, slim body stretched out across three middle seats.

I couldn't sleep. She slept the entire six and a half hours on the Lufthansa flight to Dusseldorf. We arrived at 6:00 a.m. and she had to be at an 8:00 a.m. rehearsal. She would spend the next three days on the runways at the collections known as CPD Dusseldorf, a fashion trade fair that the Igedo Company has been hosting in Germany since 1949.

I had recognized Lu while we were waiting to board. She goes by her one name as a New York model, but her full name is Lu Celania Sierra.

As soon as I saw her, even minus makeup, a cotton neckerchief knotted around her long braided hair, I recognized her from years and years of New York runway work. She's still at it.

Most memories center around Bob Mackie. She always stole the shows in which she appeared.

"Don't talk about Bob Mackie. I might cry," she said as we chatted before boarding at Kennedy International Airport.

The sadness, of course, comes from the fact Mackie, who did those colossal wardrobes for Cher and Carol Burnett, is no longer in business and doing runway shows. He always did big production numbers. In addition to wearing clothes beautifully, Lu was a little actress. The crowd loved her and the more they reacted, the more she did with that face and that slinky body and nonstop leggy legs. She's 5-feet-11 1/2.

There was one show several years ago in which she came out at the end as a French maid. Mackie always presented his collections with brief little story lines. He usually had a final scene which had photographers ya-hooing and a crowd on its feet in appreciation. Very Hollywood.

"You have no idea the nasty mail I got from other women, including black fashion writers, because I dared to be a maid."

Lu is black. That incident, she said, was startling.

"I was wearing this sexy little outfit. I doubt any maid any color ever wore anything quite so glamorous, or that short, or cut quite that low," she said, rolling her very expressive eyes.

"Do you remember when I was Billie Holiday for a finale in his show? That was the best. I got to come out in this white glittery dress, typical Mackie, and that gardenia over one ear. That was a thrill."

Two days into the shows at the Dusseldorf fair grounds, I ran into Lu again. She had already been in several shows, including Escada, Uli Schneider, Laurel and Tristano Onofri.

Vivienne Westwood was showing for the first time in Dusseldorf. Her show was coming up next when I saw Lu in the Fashion Forum foyer, sipping some mineral water.

She wasn't booked for Westwood and, she said, some other models had backed out at the last minute.

"They didn't want to wear those platform shoes she shows because you can easily fall off them and break an ankle. If you're a model who has other bookings, it's too dangerous."

We got to talking about other black models who were so popular on runways years ago. One was Billie Blair from Detroit.

She left modeling rather abruptly, at her peak. It just got to be too much for her.

"She was my idol. She's now living with her mother, and she's going to be a nurse," said Lu.

Blair was one of the most charismatic models I had ever seen, much like Naomi Sims, the Pittsburgh model who broke ground for many of the black models we see today. Both moved like gazelles and made just maneuvering a wrist to undo a button an art form.

Another popular black model was Pat Cleveland, who became one of Halston's favorites in his heyday...she of the bouncy, sexy walk and those red, red lips. Lu says Cleveland has two children and owns a boutique outside Rome.

But here was the surprise. Remember I said Lu was close to 6 feet and a size 4-6? She was once a plus-size model!

She said her admiration of Mackie goes back to his encouraging her to lose weight. He told her if she ever did she could model for him. She eventually went from size 16 and a 44 bra cup size to her present size. She's flat-chested and her legs are as thin as clothes props. In weight loss, where do the bosoms go? I can't figure that out.

PLAYTIME FOR PUCCI

July 1965

Great color, love of life, and a feeling for beauty—typical Italian traits—can easily be a summation of what a visitor might see in Florence. There's more to it than that, of course, as hundreds of Americans are discovering as they travel through European countries. People are what count.

But my trip here has given me an opportunity to observe the creative designers who are part of the fashion world. Coupled with the natural scenic vistas, it's a fine way to get a feeling for a country and its people.

Fashion is a business, whether it be in Florence, Rome, Paris, or New York. But there's time for play, too. I arrived in Florence with some fifty representatives of top magazines and newspapers to view the Florence Fashion Center shows, a trip sponsored by Braniff International Airways. Specifically, we were to view the collection of Emilio Pucci, one of Italy's most prominent designers and one name familiar to American women, too.

My inside view of Pucci, a designer, skier, art lover, scholar, and decorated Italian flyer, would catch him at play, at least temporarily.

On the roof top of the Excelsior Hotel here, a black tie dinner and a reception brought duchesses, other designers, magnificently attired society persons, political figures, and special guests. Down below, the Arno River flowed peacefully and up above, a perfect evening sky.

It was a genuine example of the continental charm of a city and its people. The breezes of the night were cool but welcome after a long day of traveling from New York to Pisa and finally, Florence, certainly one of the most romantic spots in the world.

Pucci, in private life, is Marchese di Barsento. He proudly states, "I am the first member of my family to work in a thousand years," and in his fashion career alone he has created a whole new attitude toward color and elegance.

His prices range from $2.50 for a handkerchief to $2,500 for an evening dress. In the boutique shop, which is located in his home, the Pitti Palace, a "cheap" tailored blouse can cost as much as $50. Several guests were appropriately attired in typical long Pucci gowns in colorful geometric design.

Pucci left the side of his lovely wife, Cristina, long enough to take to the dance floor when the music changed to the beat of the modern generation. He did the watusi and the frug as if he wanted the guests to know that he was full of spirit and didn't bury himself in the past and reputations of Old World ancestors.

Certainly, his women's clothes show that he is aware of the Space Age, in case anyone ever had any doubts.

One young Italian boy by the name of Lorenzo shook his head in bewilderment. "To see a man like that doing that type of dance," he murmured, almost in disbelief. And he was easily thirty years Pucci's junior. Things change, even in picturesque Florence. One young guest was Courrèges-inspired and she wore a typical outfit, right down to her open-toed, high white boots.

Even in the atmosphere of Michelangelo, quaint horse-driven carriages, Santa Maria del Flore, and Palazzo Vecchio, the urge to grow with the times is present. In fashion circles, of course, it is a necessity.

IF THE SHOE FITS

The fashion world's attention has been focused on the beautiful city of Paris during the past week.

Whether you have interest in fashion, its ins and outs, its ups and downs, or not, you can't help but fall in love with this city which boasts of the River Seine, the Champs-Elysées, Arc de Triomphe, Montmartre, boutiques, French berets, flowers, and perfume.

But before the hectic showings started, I arose on a rainy morning, had juice, croissants (a flaky, delicate breakfast roll), and coffee, then grabbed a taxi and headed for the Christian Dior establishment. The rain didn't dampen my spirits. It was a drizzle and, I thought, probably much like the spring season in Paris all the songs tell about.

My primary interest was the custom shoe salon at Dior. The door was open and I scurried in, dripping a bit from the rain but excited by my surroundings.

The salon is in a gray and white décor, very subdued and elegant. From a doorway I heard, "*Bonjour, Madame,*" and I turned to see Nadine Vandermarcq, a gracious young woman who was to tell me about the Dior shoes.

We first toured the Christian Dior boutique, and the atmosphere was heavy with anticipation of the fashion showings that would be taking place in one of the rooms Miss Vandermarcq pointed out to me.

"Everything is quite a mess," she said apologetically. Painters and carpenters were hurrying back and forth, too, readying the room for press and buyer showings of the fall and winter collection by Marc Bohan for Dior.

Miss Vandermarcq diplomatically refused to give names of custom shoe customers, but it would not be at all surprising to see the Duchess of Windsor, members of nobility, or film stars sitting in the plush gray velvet chairs. She did admit that much.

And Sophia Loren just had thirty pairs of custom shoes designed and made for a film. I asked if they would also become part of her personal wardrobe.

"Well, I should hope so," smiled Miss Vandermarcq. The Dior salon usually dresses an average of five plays and ten films per year.

Included in the Loren collection: a pair of calf-high boots in tucked pink chiffon; white vinyl boots reaching a good six inches above the knee; brocade slippers with pearls set in; black and white striped flats; shoes with lots of ostrich trim; polka dot shoes with a white gardenia at the throat, to name a few.

Miss Loren is an average size 8, "which isn't bad considering I am a size 9," laughed Miss Vandermarcq.

There was a rumor Elizabeth Taylor had brought some of her own jewels to the salon to have them put on dance slippers, but Miss Vandermarcq denied knowledge of this. In fact, it was this rumor which brought me to the salon, just to find out about such unusual requests.

I must admit, some of the shoes were the most beautiful I have ever seen. They were true works of art. I toured the boutique and then Miss Vandermarcq saw me to the door, a custom in Paris I find most pleasant.

"Please come again," she said. "And I must apologize for my country."

I wondered what she meant.

"For the rain," she smiled, shaking her head with dismay.

As if a little rain could dampen my enthusiasm for Paris.

DISHING OVER
HAMBURGERS

January 1966

Walking thirty blocks on a windy day with the temperature somewhere near 18 degrees is a breeze when the mission is to meet with Lauren Bacall. She's the star of the top comedy hit of the season on Broadway, but her role in *Cactus Flower* wasn't the reason for the meeting.

Betty Bacall, as she is known to her friends, is a fashion plate. Or maybe, "dish" might be a better word. And we were to talk about clothes.

The original plan was to meet at her apartment in the Dakota, but her schedule was a hectic one, understandably, and time was precious. We met at a tiny Hamburger Haven on Madison Avenue. What a dandy place to talk about Norman Norell's expensive clothes.

Lauren Bacall, actress, mother, and former model, is the type of woman who glamorizes anything she wears or any place she chooses to visit.

"I'm starved," she exclaimed in that familiar deep voice. "I'll have a hamburger and a hot chocolate."

It was 4:00 p.m. and this was her lunch. Asked if she usually ate before or after the show, she replied, "Both. I'm always hungry." (And she's a size 10.)

She was wearing a pale green, double-breasted coat with a matching skirt, white wool turtleneck sweater, bone-colored shoes with flattie heels, and white textured stockings. Around her head was a matching pale green chiffon headscarf.

"If the millinery business depended on me, it would be in a sorry shape," she said. "I almost never wear a hat and I love scarves."

She took a healthy bite of her hamburger. "Of course, I've always had good hair. Maybe that's the reason. And I've always worn it long. When it is much shorter, it's because the hairdresser has made a mistake."

When you visit New York, you get so used to seeing fantastically made-up faces on women, false eyelashes, four shades of eye shadow, subtle shadings of foundation, and fancy hairdos, you feel like the original paleface. Miss Bacall needs none of this cosmetic assistance. She wore no makeup at all, except for lipstick.

When the name of Norman Norell came up, Miss Bacall was almost reverent. "He's the greatest designer in the world, in my opinion," she said. "He did four outfits for me for the show and he does most of my personal wardrobe. A marvelous man.

"He could almost design all his clothes for me," she went on. "They are so right and so comfortable. After all, that's what is important in clothes, isn't it?"

At home she loves to wear pants, mostly styled by Pucci, but she hopes to have Norell do some for her. Hostess skirts, as a rule, aren't in her wardrobe.

She had three colored bands on one finger and a gold ring on her little finger. "I love rings and sometimes have them on four fingers," she said. "I love all kinds of pretty goodies, but I hate to shop. I'd like to be able to say a magic word and have all the pretty things minus the shopping chore."

FACTORY-MADE FANTASY

October 1967

There is a time for gaping and gawking. When you attend what could possibly be the most "in" party on the Hollywood social schedule this year, you can be sure there's a lot to see.

And if you can stop gawking long enough when Fred Astaire and Rock Hudson stroll by, you try to remember what they are wearing. The same goes for actresses such as Janet Leigh, Mia Farrow Sinatra, Abbe Lane, Polly Bergen, Donna Reed, and Tony Curtis's wife, Christine Kaufmann.

It started with a gathering at the home of Mr. and Mrs. Freddie Fields in Beverly Hills. The hostess was Polly Bergen, who greeted guests wearing gold silk satin hostess pajamas, designed by California designer Cardinali. Her gold and diamond jewelry was mighty impressive, too.

Miss Bergen, who just turned down five million dollars for her new cosmetic concern, Oil of the Turtle, invited fashion editors to her home for cocktails prior to visiting the discotheque of the hour, The Factory.

The fact that her husband, Freddie Fields, heads his own talent management concern had a great deal to do with the more-than-normal number of celebrities who turned out for the party.

The phrase "star-studded" could easily be considered too conservative for this party.

Nightlife in Hollywood and Beverly Hills, I'm told, is usually confined to at-home gatherings. Seldom do you see the number of celebrities that gathered at The Factory under one roof at one time.

The fact that the turtle has been money in the bank for Polly Bergen might have some connection with her husband's attire for the evening, but the white turtleneck shirt worn with sport blazer was almost a uniform among some of the men who gyrated on the small dance floor and ate snacks from the oyster bar.

Gene Barry of *Bat Masterson* fame was a turtle devotee, as was Pierre Salinger (his was pink), who is one of the owners of the dance spot, along with Paul Newman, Sammy Davis Jr., Anthony Newley, and a few others.

Jack Carter showed up at the party wearing white buckled shoes, flannel trousers, V-neck sweater, and blue shirt. Milton Berle was also sporty and his wife wore a white wool mini-dress and high black vinyl boots.

Minis and micro-minis were the order of the day for the females who couldn't seem to get enough of the wild and wonderful music.

Mia Farrow Sinatra wore a long caftan or muumuu-style frock in a sheer material, little sandals on her feet, beads around her neck. You couldn't miss that famous haircut, and Liza Minnelli, also sporting the cropped hairdo, wore a gold knitted mini-dress with long sleeves.

Henry Fonda was on the freight elevator which carried us to the top floor of The Factory, which really was a factory for bombsights at one time, according to Mr. Salinger.

The décor is fantastic, with a huge in-the-round fireplace at one end, a room with billiard tables in the back, stained-glass windows in every pattern providing the roof over the dance area.

Sonny and Cher were there, too. They looked like transplanted Indians in their buckskin ensembles, which Cher designed.

Fred Astaire was conservative in slacks, shirt, sport jacket and tie, quite a contrast to Steve McQueen wearing white trousers and an orange see-through shirt, beads around his neck. Even larger beads were worn by Freddie Brisson, film producer and husband of Rosalind Russell.

Miss Russell, by the way, was the surprise of the evening; she wore the tunic top from a black lace and beaded pants ensemble in which she made her entrance in the film *Auntie Mame.*

Steve McQueen's wife, one of the best dancers on the floor, wore a purple shimmery micro-mini (that means bathing-suit length) and the sheer material revealed a bra of rhinestones with thin rhinestone straps.

Her husband, by the way, eventually added yellow ski or motorcycle goggles...the better to find his partner, perhaps.

Janet Leigh wore a black slip of a sequined dress, mini also, and long rope pearls which swung wildly when she danced. Actress Barbara Rush appeared in a purple chiffon Nina Ricci with can-can petticoats underneath in four or five colors.

Donna Reed wore conservative pink satin and Abbe Lane was in a white wool tent dress banded in gold.

Everything goes for attire at a place like The Factory. The clothes were fun. The party was fun. Surely it was a thrill to see Fred Astaire approach the dance floor with Judy Garland's daughter, Liza, on his arm, but the floor was so crowded they barely did one full box step.

Somehow, all the minis, glitter dresses, pantsuits, turtlenecks and wildly colored stockings make sense in this atmosphere. Watching a star like Roz Russell try her sense of rhythm with today's generation of swingers only solidified an already well-known fact: Age is a state of mind.

RAZZLE DAZZLE ROZ

October 1967

It was my birthday and meeting Rosalind Russell was probably the nicest thing that could have happened to me. Particularly when she gave me a big hug and wished me many happy returns of the day.

There she was in the restaurant at Universal City, greeting fashion editors, shaking hands, posing for photographs, and answering strange questions.

"What is your favorite flower, Miss Russell?" That was one such query. And later: "What do you think of all the actors going into politics?"

Well, in trying to angle questions toward fashion, my most immediate thought was about her skirt lengths. After all, that's what most women talk about these days, whether they are at bridge club, having a second cup of coffee at a drugstore counter, at the beauty parlor, or as in this case, at a film studio facing an actress who has always been associated with glamour.

She's a star to the hilt.

Miss Russell was wearing a white wool dress by James Galanos, possibly the most famous of the West Coast designers. He also has been doing most of Mrs. Ronald Reagan's clothes. The skirt length was about one inch above the knee.

"This length is a bit short," she confided, "but when Jimmy sold it to me, he said it should not be lengthened. First of all, on a white dress it shows."

The actress, who has always been a star but is possibly remembered for her Auntie Mame portrayal, is in a new movie called *Rosie* and she'll have another opportunity to wear a stupendous wardrobe by another West Coast great, Jean Louis.

Before we enjoyed a buffet dinner high on a hill with the San Fernando Valley spread out below us like one massive blanket of glittering diamonds, a full moon overhead, we viewed a short film used to test wardrobes to be worn by Miss Russell and Sandra Dee, who is also in the Ross Hunter production.

Portraying the richest woman in the world, Rosalind Russell wears an expensive wardrobe, naturally, and the studio heads were anxious to point out "all the jewelry is the real thing" …not that I would ever know the difference. I am sure, however, the magnificent brooch, earrings, and bracelet worn by Miss Russell this particular evening were real.

The one thing that caught my eye immediately was the small clutch purse she carried. The "clutch" was really a hand warmer, she said, which she had gotten in the Himalayas. I couldn't help but think of Auntie Mame wandering all over the world. It was just the type of gadget she might have purchased on one of her jaunts.

"Look," she said, "how much it holds." And with that she opened the square metal box that resembled a small pillow with a jade clasp and revealed her compact, a cigarette lighter, and two or three other items. "I've had it for twenty years," she said. "Almost as long as I've been married. It will be twenty-six years this month, by the way."

There has been a great deal of conversation lately concerning the new musical play *Coco*, based on the life of Paris designer Gabrielle Chanel.

Miss Russell has been announced as the lead and her husband, Freddie Brisson, is to produce the show. Chanel, however, has been quoted as saying she wants Katharine Hepburn to play the role.

162

Miss Russell wasn't making any commitments concerning the controversy, but if and when the play is produced it seems likely she will play Coco.

"If I do it," she stated, "it would not be until next year."

When I chatted with Miss Russell and mentioned Pittsburgh, she thought for a moment and said, "Ah yes, the Nixon Theater." It was in 1952 she appeared there in *Bell, Book and Candle.*

Clothes have always played a big part in Rosalind Russell's life and probably because she is the type of woman who has flair. On the other hand, if she isn't parading in glitter at-home pajamas, carrying a long cigarette holder å la Mame Dennis, she could be portraying a nun, a wild personality such as in *Oh Dad, Poor Dad,* or a Jewish widow from Brooklyn in *A Majority of One.*

Mrs. Jean Louis mingled with the party group as did Sandra Dee, the latter wearing a white silk crepe dress trimmed with glitter (a dress which she confessed was not a Jean Louis) covered with a fox fur coat, her blond hair heightened with many fake curls.

Mrs. Louis (pronounced "Louee") wore a black theater suit covered in jet black and sequin beading.

By the way, Miss Russell's favorite flower is white lilac and she's all in favor of actors going into politics if they are qualified. She admitted, however, she had no leanings in that direction.

Anyone who cares to guess Miss Russell's age is free to do so, but to me she is ageless. Her attire for this occasion was elegant and yet it was new. Her hemline was short, but not overly so, and her T-strap shoes were low heeled and flattering to her very slim legs.

Films are make-believe, but I'm happy to say Rosalind Russell is real.

STYLISH PATRIOTISM

March 1968

The White House held its first fashion show.

Although fashion shows and luncheons have become as much a part of the American woman's way of life as lipsticks and hairnets, this one had a distinctly different flavor.

First of all, Mrs. Lyndon Johnson was the hostess.

Another "can you top this" extra was the appearance of the president himself, who stood under a portrait of Lincoln and said he had been in conferences all morning, "but there are so many governors in town, I didn't want to leave the White House too long."

He continued, "All our talk has been of housing, foreign policy, and welfare, and I thought I'd leave for a while, see all of you, and then take my nap."

He gave daughter Lynda a kiss on the cheek as he left the room.

For good measure, the U. S. Marine Band supplied music from the adjoining foyer.

No model has ever made an entrance on a runway in such grand style.

And luncheon wasn't just the traditional chicken à la king, but chicken curry Columbus. The menu, table centerpieces, and outfits worn by Mrs. Johnson's staff waved the American flag, quietly, of course, in a color scheme of red, white, and blue.

It was definitely a day to feel thrilled, chilled, and trembly, agreed the usually cool, calm, and sophisticated models flown in from New York.

"I don't know, it's just marvelous," said tall, dark-haired Denise Linden, one of New York's most elegant mannequins.

"I don't think anything I've ever done matches this," she said, grasping in her hand some of the patriotic banners she and the other girls carried in the fashion show. "I'm taking these home for my children," she said proudly.

"After all, just think of history books and all that has taken place in the White House. And there I am having fittings in Lincoln's bedroom."

Models weren't the only ones who were impressed with the grand atmosphere of the First Family's official residence.

There were twenty-five of America's top designers represented in the show. Some well-known names, such as Geoffrey Beene and Oscar de La Renta, were unable to attend due to bad weather conditions in New York. Mollie Parnis and Adele Simpson, two of Mrs. Johnson's favorites, suffered the same fate as fog closed the airport.

Norman Norell was in Palm Beach and couldn't make it, James Galanos is in Europe. Donald Brooks is in Hollywood, Jacques Tiffeau and milliner Adolfo were absent.

But it didn't matter. The excitement of the whole afternoon was mixed with patriotic fervor. Nobody knows exactly why a fashion show has never been held at the White House before, but everyone felt this one was worth waiting for.

Rudi Gernreich, California designer, sat at a table with Lynda Bird. Texan designer John Moore arrived from Palm Beach and Sydney Wragge stopped over on his way to Boca Raton, Florida. Mr. Moore designed Mrs. Johnson's inaugural gown.

"This is a great thing for the American fashion industry being officially recognized," said Don Simonelli, one of this country's newest talents on the designing scene.

He admitted that he was acting like a schoolboy with the wonder of it all. "Imagine, sitting in the White House and watching my clothes on a runway," he said, shaking his head in disbelief.

The star-studded luncheon audience, politically speaking, included wives of governors who are here attending the annual conference, and wives of cabinet members.

Mrs. Nelson Rockefeller, wearing a pink wool gabardine dress, sat at a table next to Mrs. Henry H. Fowler, wife of the secretary of the Treasury. Mrs. Hubert H. Humphrey, wife of the vice president, was wearing all white, as was Mrs. Johnson.

Pauline Trigère, French-born American designer, wore red and was at Mrs. Johnson's table. Mrs. Winthrop A. Rockefeller, wife of the Arkansas governor, also wore red. Designers Chester Weinberg, Herbert Levine, Jerry Silverman, George Stavropoulos, and William Travilla were spotted at various tables.

A special runway was built in the State Dining Room where the event was held. At the other end of the hallway is the East Room where Lynda Bird's wedding took place.

Mrs. Johnson showed obvious delight the fashion show tied in so nicely with the travel-in-America program, which her husband has encouraged. She smiled constantly.

While models showed the works of talented designers, slides were flashed on a screen behind the runway depicting America's tourist spots. All the luncheon guests received hand-screened scarves which said "Discover America."

It was definitely a flag-waving day, but nobody seemed to mind. The White House is definitely the place to do it.

PLAYMATE AT THE MANSION

January 1991

Wow, what a week! Spending time in La-La Land, or Los Angeles environs, has its moments. Not only was I presented a Lifetime Achievement Award from the Men's Fashion Association, which came as a surprise and made me wonder if I was going into forced retirement, but I think I spotted Kevin Costner. I know I spotted Michael Douglas. Not at the awards show, but at Spago, a trendy restaurant.

And—if you can envision this—I mingled with Hugh Hefner's bunnies on the grounds of his Playboy mansion. Not the female bunnies, but real bunnies.

We read so much about Hefner's lifestyle and beautiful women, but now with the demise of the Playboy Club's bunny-waitresses with the puffy white tails and low decolleté, Hefner has become a naturalist. He has live bunnies roaming the acreage, along with a bevy of magnificent white flamingos, monkeys, ducks, and other animals and birds. It's awesome.

I asked if they worry that the bunnies and ducks might run or fly away.

The answer: "Why would they want to? Would you leave this place?"

Good point.

The grounds of Hefner's Holmby Hills mansion prove he loves nature. But there's a dichotomy. Even as you enter from the driveway, you walk past guards and a security station, two caged fluffy sheep dogs…and a Pepsi vending machine.

The party was hosted by Allyn Saint George, a menswear designer who took the opportunity to announce he has added coats to his licensed items. He couldn't have picked a flashier way to do it.

Our bus passed houses as big as hotels and pulled into the Playboy driveway. We got out and walked past Jaguars and Rolls-Royces until an outdoor fantasyland exploded into view. With a waterfall, no less. There is a "lagoon" of clear blue water slithering through the grounds, up and under huge rocks. In the middle is Hefner's sauna. You just swim right into it, completely obscured but still in a natural setting. And around the hot tub are soft cushions and chaises where, I imagine, you can sweat to your heart's content. Or sip champagne…whatever.

The Hefner workout room and his game room are bigger and more complete than most commercial spas. He even has his star in a walkway path around the side of the mansion, just like the Hollywood Walk of Fame.

Hefner wasn't part of the party. He just allowed three hundred guests to walk around the estate, nibble incredible hors d'oeuvres, and have drinks from three bars.

The interior of the mansion was off-limits, but walking around I looked in one room with huge windows and confirmed the house was lived in.

There were a number of baby carriers—a stroller, a car seat, some toys scattered about. This is new for mansion décor. Hef became a new daddy last April at age 64.

A Playboy executive told me Hefner bought the house in 1971 for $1.5 million and put another $10 million into development of the grounds.

On a clear night, through the trees, you can see the well-lighted mansion producer Aaron Spelling has been building for the past four years. Rumor has it Hefner's place will pale by comparison in opulence. Is that possible?

Consider the house Spelling bought in 1984 was $10.5 million, and Spelling once traveled coast to coast on his own private railroad car with a dining room which seated twelve.

This new estate, even more elaborate, is already a sightseeing attraction. I heard there were forty-five rooms. After all, someone said, you have to remember there will be three people living there.

WAVES OF CHANGE

August 1999

Yes, Stone Harbor again. What is it now? I count fifty-two years. I'd like to think that means I started coming here in diapers, but alas, no. My first year was 1947, and I was all grown up. Or so I thought.

The gulls still amaze me with their grace; I still wander through Hoy's 5&10 as if I was at Nordstrom; the salt air still revitalizes me in a way I can never describe.

Harry Otto continues to sweep the pole net across the pool to keep it clean and sparkling at the Lark Motel. He raises the flag each morning, greets the truck with the clean linens each day as he has done for more years than I can remember.

He dons his latex gloves and performs his tasks diligently, taking time to discuss a book he has read, a play he has seen, or where the planets are rising and falling, as in your horoscope. He also plays the piano.

Families ride bikes together, have breakfast at the Pancake House or on the motel deck under an umbrella, and then take part in the town's nighttime ritual: standing in line for ice cream at Springer's, even in the humid 90-degree temperatures.

The town's island street dividers are planted colorfully and homes are, well, that's where things they are a-changin', and I mean big time.

After the usual pleasantries, conversations this year eventually got around to real estate. Which house was Oprah's? Had you seen the "marble house"?

If you can believe all that you hear, Oprah Winfrey visited the area last summer, and now it is rumored that she bought a house, the one with purple curtains, the one she rented last year. Or maybe it's one nearby. She was seen at the rented house last year "on the upper deck, wearing a bathrobe." So the gossip goes.

Another person will tell you, no, she bought a house "up in Avalon," which is the connecting resort town. It was in the newspaper. It must be true. Nobody remembered when, but somebody saw it. Did they? Who knows? Oprah Winfrey, it seems, has a vicarious connection to Stone Harbor, whether she owns a house or not.

My guess is, she does not. The visit last summer is likely true. People saw her shopping on 96th Street. It doesn't mean she bought a house.

Whether she did or didn't isn't the point. Just thinking she might have gives people something to do. You can be at the beach just so long, and you can play miniature golf just so many times. But I will tell you this: It would seem only people with her kind of money can build or buy in what was once a modest town.

One evening I stood in front of a real estate office with a "talking" window. You punch in the numbers of a house pictured and you get vitals, like the price. The very modest one I inquired about was $339,000, and I was told it was probably a "TD" (tear-down).

Homes being built are priced out of sight. In the millions, side street or beach front, decks on every level and off every room, and an attempt to re-create Tara, pillars and all. It's staggering. My Aunt Edna had bought a small cottage here in the late '50s. It cost $6,000.

Enter the marble dwelling in Avalon. No, it's not Oprah's. I don't think I spoke to a soul who didn't ask if I had seen it yet.

Finally, after dinner my last night, my cousin Lynn said, "Let's go see the marble house."

I was dumbfounded. The $339,000 house I had seen could have served as the doghouse, except it wasn't marble.

I would prefer none of this flashy lifestyle and celebrity had come to my beloved ocean retreat, which once had mostly shingled and shuttered houses, screened-in porches, and no landscaping—just twining honeysuckle going wild, or unpruned hydrangea bushes. This little piece of heaven has been discovered, unfortunately, and there's no stopping the "progress."

Do those who own such homes still find pleasure in just bringing home a seashell, sand in their shoes, and maybe some saltwater taffy? I wonder.

I'll always have my own memories shared with family in a tiny rented cottage by the sea, three in a bed, fresh crabs on the kitchen table, and lots and lots of laughter.

The day I left, Harry surprised me with a gift. It was a candle trimmed with seashells. I had seen the marble house. The candle, however, made me feel I was a lot richer than the people who lived there.

SOUND BYTES AT THE CARNEGIE

February 2000

Wouldn't it be fun to record remarks made by those of us who peruse, ponder, and procrastinate as we move through the various offerings at the Carnegie International?

We might sound as ignorant as novices, but perhaps we also would be insightful.

When I read what is behind an artist's presentation, I often wonder if it isn't just so much intellectualizing. The reasoning often seems so deep, we feel inferior if we don't get it.

Why not allow onlookers to go cold turkey? No well-written brochures allowed. Sometimes, my initial impression might be similar to the artist's explanation, but more often it was not.

On the day a friend and I toured the CI, we would often hear visitors remark: "What do you think that is?"

We'd be thinking the same.

"Is that part of the show or did someone break a window?"

"Are those meant to resemble cow udders? I think they are stretched-out pantyhose."

Great sound bytes.

My friend and I didn't expect to understand all that we saw, but we felt it was a happening. We wanted some culture. We also wanted an excuse to have lunch at an Oakland bistro and catch up on gossip.

A quickie trek through the halls of The Carnegie, and that would be that. I'd order the California salad. Should I have wine?

That's probably the wrong preface to a CI experience, but it's honest.

Here's more honesty. We began to enjoy it. The salad (and wine) were on hold.

We gawked, admired, questioned, passed by, debunked, stared at, and questioned as we strolled. Now that's pretty darn good, I think. We were stimulated. I guess that's as much as you can ask of any kind of exhibition, play, symphony, or opera performance.

Some insist on having a docent explain what it is they are looking at and, in turn, possibly direct them emotionally in terms of what they are supposed to feel.

My friend and I read explanations in the brochure from time to time, usually after we had assessed a piece of work, giggled at it, or felt lost in trying to figure out just what the heck it was supposed to relate.

We were also in awe more than once. We wanted to know more. There we were, just average albeit gorgeous women, without much in the way of expectations.

As I said, we poked fun at times, but we also marveled at the patience and the imagination of some of the artists.

You are allowed to giggle. This is America.

We would not have known that Chris Ofili used elephant dung if we hadn't been told. Could have been just plain mud. Or papier-maché.

I kept trying to envision these people, how they spend an ordinary day doing ordinary things, when their minds race and envision, then they follow through by actually building such…such…well, such things.

We removed our shoes and walked through the stretched-out gauzy sculpture, as invited.

I got woozy. I doubt that was the intent. Slight movement tends to affect my balance at times. Walking "on air" was not pleasant, so I exited quickly. My experience. Probably not yours.

The mind works in mysterious ways. I was reminded of my migraines.

The crisscross Ping-Pong tables (table tennis to the elite) and the pond in the middle were thought-provoking. Was it art? At least it made me wonder and smile. I haven't thought about Ping-Pong since our family tournaments years ago, before television. We were competitive. I had a mean backhand.

The dripping beads of water on the white wall? Reminded me of my whitewashed basement wall that used to "bleed" during heavy rains.

The program says it represents "the body in all its vulnerability."

I wasn't even close.

We bring so much of ourselves to someone else's creation.

I pulled into my garage the other day.

There were stacks of leftover deck slats, piled this way and that, cracked clay pots with dried-up summer foliage, a jug of car coolant, and a forlorn bird feeder no longer capable of providing a refuge for the sparrows.

Hmmm. Was this art?

What did it say?

It says clean out the garage.

GREEN THUMBS UP

May 2003

Throughout the spring, not just today, I think of my mother most often, and it is when I am most like her, I think. It's when I'm working in the garden.

In her lifetime, she had no idea her youngest daughter would become a gardener. I use the term loosely but lovingly.

As I have grown older, I have found the dirt under my finger-nails to be the crowning achievement of my senior years. It's the reason I will probably stay in my house as long as I can bend and not even consider living in an apartment.

I need to garden. I don't think of it as a chore. I don't think of it as a hobby. I am compelled, driven by an energy I seldom can muster to change my bed linens or tackle the kitchen cupboards.

I can lose a day in the garden. I'm not that good at it, under-stand. I'm not even sure my mother was a know-how gardener.

She never took classes. I never saw her poring over garden books. I don't recall her being specific about tall plants in the back and shorter ones in the front. She didn't consider the landscape; she just planted. Perhaps it's a case of having a green thumb. Mine is sore, if not green.

What I remember is my mother on her knees, putting her flowers in their beds with such care.

It's a strong image, much like seeing her at the dining-room table wrapping Christmas gifts with such distinction and patience. It's etched in memory.

When I was young, I used to go with her to get the new plants, just about my only contribution to our garden array.

There was a farmer on the outskirts of Uniontown named

Melvin. He was always tanned and dressed in coveralls and a straw hat, spending most of his days tending to the vegetables and flowers from which he made his living. He was a true farmer, proud and pleasant.

We went there for his lima beans, peas and beets and berries, as well as flowers, which usually meant loading the trunk of the car with sweet peas, columbine, petunias, snapdragons, and baby's breath.

I admit, at the time I did not know the names of the flowers we were purchasing. I just knew they were pretty.

There was no Kmart or Home Depot garden center, not even on the drawing boards. Still, my mother's garden was lush.

I worry that I never told her it was beautiful.

The old standbys were comforting each year, and whatever my mother did, with or without an expert's advice, she managed to cheer up any backyard.

I remember them best from three houses where we lived as I grew up. Our houses and yards became smaller as we moved and aged, but we were never without flowers. A fresh bouquet was always on the piano.

The nice thing is remembering her joy. She seemed to escape the day's problems, even when my father was serving in New Guinea during World War II, by heading for the garden.

I imagine tears were shed there. It was often after dark.

I know, because I do that as well.

My mother never had sculpted nails, although for special occasions she did clean up nicely and wear nail polish. It was her pleasure, digging in the dirt. I had no idea it would someday be mine as well.

I don't wear gloves, nor did my mother. I often swoosh up something sharp, which means I am picking away at splinters in my fingers many evenings. I don't know when my nails last saw polish. The splinters are my badges of honor. I have some arthritis in my hands. My mother had it, too, and in her knees.

But even with a short jab of pain from time to time as I tug at ivy or lift a heavy planter, I take great joy in the pain. I know I'm alive.

Once a selfish teenager concerned only with washing my hair and having a date on Saturdays, I can't believe today I am often asked the name of a plant or which ones do well in shade.

I've given up the Saturday night dates. There's just so little time when you are a gardener! You have to make choices.

I describe my garden space as postage-stamp, meaning quite small compared to greater gardens with far more variety and expert arrangements of exotic flowers.

I tend to try some new things, but I select most varieties, especially pansies, because mother always planted them. She said I used to hold the flowers between my fingers and talk to them as a little girl.

I wish my mother could have seen me become her, on my knees, in a garden, nails full of dirt, wishing the day could be longer but eager for the next morning when I can do it all over again. I somehow inhaled her joy and kept some of what she had found so many years ago as my very own.

I miss her, but I need only pick up my trowel and begin to dig. She's right beside me.

EVERYONE WORE WHITE

May 2007

Weddings. There are millions of them. And each has its own story.

For the many years I have been writing for newspapers I have described my fair share of weddings in print. By its very nature, this won't be like any of those.

I had watched my son, Drew, walk across scattered rose petals on the sandy beach at Cabo San Lucas in Mexico, then turn to await his bride. He looked so confident, this child of mine, standing there in his off-white linen suit and open-collared white shirt, but mostly he just looked happy. He had eyes only for another woman. Her name is Maggie.

Where did my little boy go? Was it time to lapse into a lyric from the song in *Mame*, in which she asks that question as she sees her nephew Patrick all grown up?

My son has literally grown up in my writings the past thirty-six years. Now he has found the love of his life. Can a mother ask for more?

Anyone who sees a child married can identify with what my heart is saying. It is not unique. We travel back in time—years—in a matter of minutes.

It was a destination wedding, a new term for me. They wanted to celebrate their love in a nontraditional setting with those who have been most important in their lives.

If you didn't feel love in this atmosphere, your heart wasn't pumping.

Such a wedding can take as much time and effort as any traditional wedding. You are dealing with a different language, long-distance communication, airline delays, new passport confusion, and the unforeseen.

At the rehearsal dinner, a guest, Liz Mulvihill, tripped, resulting in a ride to the hospital with a small foot fracture. The good news, she made it to the wedding the next day, albeit in a wheelchair!

One month ago today, April 7, Drew Harlan Cloud took Margaret Marie Garcia as his bride. Why Cabo? They wanted to be married on a beach, and if it couldn't be Stone Harbor, New Jersey, Mexico was bueno.

Close friends and family had said, "Tell us where and when and we'll be there." And indeed, fifty-six people gathered for swimming, golfing, lounging, eating, tanning, and catching up—all in three days before the exchange of vows.

My son's two half-brothers, one with his wife and three children, and his half-sister shared the adventure. I was touched beyond words by their presence.

There were friends from elementary school, high school, college, and the workplace. Drew and Maggie both work for the NBA Phoenix Suns.

Wardrobe and the age-old "what to wear" dilemma was solved when Maggie asked everyone to wear white for the wedding.

I chose a white peasant skirt and flutter-sleeve crochet top and already had the silver belt and sandals. Bueno again!

There aren't many weddings where you can wear rubber flip-flops, but this was one of them. In fact such footwear was required for the surprise reception held on a yacht, the *Orion*.

The bride wore a long, slim, ivory silk charmeuse gown she had picked out last summer. That was the dress, she said, as soon as she saw it online from Nordstrom. She never wavered.

When she reached the beach after descending a steep and winding walkway on the arm of her father, she simply removed her high heels. Many guests also carried their shoes. It was difficult to walk in the sand.

A Mexican musician softly played the harp.

We were asked to close our eyes and listen to the sounds around us on a glorious sun-drenched afternoon, white surf slapping against the huge rocks in front of us. It was God's infinite church, minus roof, pews and stained glass, but so spiritual.

A few gulls flew over the blue-green Sea of Cortez highlighted by white foam edges, the white fabric-covered chairs, guests in their cool white attire—but they seemed respectful and soared quietly to the heavens as if in musical sync with the soft clear voice singing "Ave Maria."

On one of Drew's fingers was the ring I had seen on my late father's hand all my life. Caressing Maggie's middle finger was my late mother's engagement ring. A diamond belonging to her late grandmother sparkled at the hollow of her neck.

Drew and Maggie's one disappointment: They forgot to bring their Pittsburgh Steelers Terrible Towel to the ceremony. They have taken it along and photographed it every step of the way during their four-year courtship, including the night he proposed, last July 7, on Mount Washington.

The wedding was the day before Easter. It marks a new beginning.

And Mother's Day is Sunday. This year I am proud to say I have a son, as always, but now I am also blessed with a daughter.

"I appeared on your Nixon stage many times and walked through your park many times after a show…sometimes with a heavy heart, sometimes with a very glad heart."

—Katharine Cornell, 1961

"I started as a singer and I believe it was right here in Pittsburgh I made my second professional appearance at Carnegie Hall."

—Walter Pidgeon, 1959

"I cook my husband's breakfast every morning, but admit I use too much butter and he has to watch his weight. When you are happily married, you take time to be with your husband."

—Joan Crawford, 1958

"I came from a family which was small by Greek standards—just five kids. But the first out of the house was always the best dressed."

—Telly Savalas, 1974

"I was a student at Carnegie Tech, and I was a night janitor, taught fencing, and spent Sundays announcing for WLOA in Braddock."

—George Peppard, 1960

When

THE STREET WHERE YOU LIVE

November 1963

What does your street look like?

Mine is shaded with maple trees. It isn't a very long street. It doesn't have mansions or landscaped lawns and people must park their cars in front of their houses. It is a paved street, and at one end there is a slight rise resembling a hill.

The only things that have changed in the past twenty years are a few residents and some coats of paint on the houses. There might be an additional picture window or two and maybe a front porch has given way to a more modern wrought-iron railing. But otherwise this is the street where I lived.

Oh, not literally. My family lived a couple of streets away and that's where I cuddled in a nice warm bed at night and sat on a swing on our back porch. This was home. But I "lived" my growing-pain years on the street with the maple trees. My best friend lived on this street, too.

I lived there as most youngsters do. Young people find a street where they can play, a street where there are other boys and girls who ride bicycles, roller skate, and play games. Some very happy days are spent so, in summer and fall.

Sometimes we just sat on a curbstone and talked. The subject didn't matter. It might not have been anything more important than a decision to use only one skate the next time down the hill.

If you see it every day, you might not think twice about it. And maybe it is a bit silly to become sentimental about a street.

Hometowns revisited always bring on gushy reminiscences and periods of nostalgic remember-when. Houses where you used to live bring on the same flow of memories, some sad and not so pleasant, but others that cause you to smile.

I never fail to walk or ride just a bit slower past the house where my grandfather lived. Do I really remember that he carried me on his shoulders, or did another tell me the story so often that I can almost see him coming down the walk?

And the house with the chicken coop in back that was the dollhouse. You wonder what they use it for now. You recall how the front of the house was decorated for Christmas. And the window at the side of the house that was used more than once when you forgot your key.

If someone had asked me as a ten-year-old to describe the street where I played as a youngster, I'm sure it would have sounded something like this: It is very, very steep…It takes great skill to skate down from the top…It is very wide and spacious…The trees are giants and it takes years to learn to climb them.

Just the other day I drove to the street that had provided me with so many pleasant memories. I couldn't believe it was so small and the hill just a lift or two higher than the flat road. I suddenly felt very old.

The foundation at the top of the street where we dug in the mud and created masterful roadways for miniature cars now has a house on the property. The huge tree in which I sat an entire day in order to watch a nest of robin's eggs is, in the calm light of maturity, a very small tree that takes less proficiency to climb than I imagined.

Even if supermarkets, shopping centers, parking lots, and gas stations have found roots on your childhood playground, you can close your eyes and take a sentimental journey backwards into time.

THIS LADY WAS A SCAMP

March 1990

Some people might be embarrassed to pull up to valet parking in a 1972 Plymouth Scamp. This car was tired. Worn out. Rusting. Much like its owner. Until last Monday that was me.

Never did I find it beneath my station to drive that gold beauty. I was not dry-eyed when I left the Goodwill building on the South Side, where I left my friend. My friend, the Scamp.

I donated the car. I walked away with a rusted license plate—not much after eighteen years.

I cursed it more than once. Dead batteries. A leak under the dashboard. A broken adjustment handle on the seat. An oil light that kept flashing for ten years. The arm rests were wrapped with electrical tape to hold them to the doors.

It was on its last legs two years ago so I went car shopping. Though I managed to purchase a car with more going for it than sentiment, I held onto the Scamp. My son drove it to school and to work last summer. Someone whacked the driver's front door a year ago so it was a bit curled around the edges—and rusting. But it worked.

More than once I was aware of double takes when I pulled up at the dry cleaner or at the Giant Eagle. Pssst. That's the fashion editor at the *Pittsburgh Press*.

But even with my new Nissan I often drove the Scamp because I liked the bench seat far better than buckets, and my dog liked it better, too. The first ride in the Nissan he jumped from the back to the front seat and landed on the brake stick. Ouch.

When I finally said farewell to the old buggy, I was feeling close to my father. The car had been his and when I began to drive it in 1978 it had just 16,000 miles on the odometer. I added another 36,000.

Funny, but as long as I had the car I felt his presence. I could see him sitting behind the wheel, driving oh, so slowly, down Main Street. But he took great pride in never having an accident and always keeping the car in good condition. My first trip to the beach with my infant son was in that car. I see his grandma sitting in the back seat handing out fried chicken and the ham and cheese sandwiches she fixed for the trip.

My father wouldn't have liked the way old Scamp looked as I left it at Goodwill, but he would have smiled at my determination to keep driving it the twelve years since he died. He liked resourcefulness.

As I looked for the car title, I found some of his letters, written in the three years after my mother died. He was living alone, trying to make life mean something without her. And he was somewhat frightened because of his own ill health.

But he wrote beautifully. I found myself reaching for one letter after the other, feeling as if we were having a conversation. They were just about the weather and what he had for lunch and whether he had taken his walk. And how he was looking forward to our weekend visit.

The writing became more difficult to read as the letters' postmarks got closer to August 1978, but even the day before he died he recorded his confused thoughts. I ache because I can't read the scribbling.

I was feeling that ache as I drove his car to the South Side.

I had to call AAA to charge the battery to get it there—one last-gasp effort. Kind of, so long, buddy, it's time.

Just a lot of rusting metal and chrome. But I saw people I loved sitting on those black vinyl seats. You don't give that up without pause. Then you get on with things.

WAY TO GO, HARLEY

September 1991

Whether to putz or party is always a dilemma.

In my usual way, I putzed during a recent week's vacation. You see, all fashion writers do not spend leisure hours on the Riviera or in fashion salons. I've never been to the Riviera. And it's a myth fashion writers get their clothes free. For starters, the newspaper's ethics policy forbids it. But people continue to ask me if I get my clothes—anything I want—for nothing. Sometimes they may look like giveaways, but believe me, they're not.

But back to the vacation. I was not without projects. I cleaned closets, drawers, the basement, the dryer's filter screen, the bathroom medicine chest. And I hung my shingle. Actually, it's my father's shingle.

Having just seen *The Doctor*, I was feeling a bit moody about my father, who was a small town obstetrician and general practitioner. We never had a house or a car like William Hurt's in the movie.

General practitioner really is a catchall term. It means my father was a doctor who also held hands well after midnight, practiced common sense psychology, and had a strong shoulder and a quality of patience not learned in medical school. The movie about a doctor who has lost his bedside manner as he becomes successful reminded me of the differences from my father. Daddy was successful in a way that had nothing to do with money. He didn't see it that way, but when I see his name on the shingle, with office hours underneath, the dark oak frame slightly chipped and the brown paper backing so old it is cracking, I could not be more proud if he had been Jonas Salk or Thomas Starzl.

The shingle came from the office where he tended patients for at least fifty years.

After he died I retrieved it from a cabinet in the basement and hung it in his grandson's room. It was there for about twelve years ...until now.

I hoped it would give my son a sense of who his grandfather was. No matter how many posters of basketball and football greats (and *Sports Illustrated* swimsuit models) covered the bedroom walls, the shingle always had a space. But now Drew is in college, and I want the shingle to inspire me. As I hammered it into the kitchen wall, staring at the name—a name I carry proudly—I began to cry. I hit my thumb with the hammer, but the lump in the throat told me my heart had been hit as well.

During my father's last illness, and also my mother's, I met doctors who seemed more preoccupied with their new Mercedes than with the ailments they were describing—much like the character William Hurt portrays, whose story was taken from Dr. Ed Rosenbaum's book, *A Taste of My Own Medicine.*

When you trust a doctor, and they take time to know your name and maybe your favorite flower, healing beyond the textbooks begins. Milton Harlan Cloud taught me that, and I am reminded of it every time I glance toward my kitchen doorway. And I think, "Way to go, Harley."

BITE OF THE BIG APPLE

November 1994

We all need a shot in the arm every so often. Not literally, but we need something to get us excited, our adrenalin pumping.

For me that usually means a trip to New York City—which is vital if you have toiled in the fashion or theater worlds. I hate it. I love it.

I haven't been there for almost two years. I went recently to reacquaint myself with much of what I took for granted for so many years. And my adrenalin was pumping almost from the moment the plane landed and a limo driver and an attendant at the cab stand began to argue about whose fare I would be.

I'm in the middle of the vocal blasts, ignored as if what I wanted, as the prospective passenger, had no place in the argument.

"I'm in New York," I thought to myself. "Nothing has changed."

When I graduated from college I headed for New York to find my fame and fortune in the theater. Ha. That never happened. But I saw New York in a way that stayed with me.

I still try to go back to old haunts—if they are there. That includes the old Barbizon Hotel for Women, where I stayed for $30 a week. My parents were willing to pay that huge amount because it was a safe haven for their youngest daughter. Boys weren't allowed above the lobby floor.

Much changes. Much remains the same.

On buses (I use them a lot), you must still use coins for the $1.25 fare. People still push and shove.

Black is the chic clothing color. Wear all black and you are a New Yorker. Tourists will ask you for directions.

I sat on the steps surrounding the fountain in front of The

Plaza Hotel and listened to a great New Orleans jazz group. It's the same spot where I watched Barbra Streisand and Robert Redford filming *The Way We Were* many years ago.

I also went back to my favorite small hotel, The Wyndham on 58th, where I had stayed for many years but from which I was banned after I complained when I arrived one fall and my confirmed reservation was ignored.

It was the weekend of the New York marathon, probably twelve years ago, and people there for the race hadn't checked out and the hotel policy is that it can't toss them out.

Anyhow, I was back. I used to feel this hotel was a well-kept secret. It was old (1926), it was inexpensive, and it had a certain charm and friendliness, which is what kept me going back.

Donald Trump obviously hasn't noticed it yet. Each time I go to New York I expect it to be gone, or worse, turned into a pink marble palace.

When I checked in, I did not see the familiar telephone operator (she always reminded me of the character Lily Tomlin created) but it doesn't mean the hotel has gone modern. There was just a new face sitting there behind the tiny counter, plugging in and chatting with the desk clerk as she wrote down messages for guests.

Televisions do not have remotes, not even in a suite. Men will hate this hotel.

Everyone there, from the elevator operator (yes, a human being takes you to your floor) to those at the front desk and the bellhops, speak almost reverently of the late Jessica Tandy, who still had the penthouse there with her husband, Hume Cronyn, when she passed away a few weeks ago.

"A great lady, a great lady. Wonderful people," said the clerk as he handed me my key. No, it's not a card you insert in the door but a huge key that doesn't fit easily into a small evening purse.

So, I'm home, in a way. I never wanted to live in New York, even when I resided there temporarily while I waited to be discovered for the Broadway stage. But I do sense the vitality, the energy, the diversity, the style that comes walking toward you on the upper East Side, or while you are touring Barneys, the trendy new place to spend your bucks.

Imagine my surprise when, as I perused the clothing on the seventh floor, I heard a voice ask, "Aren't you Barbara Cloud?"

Discovered at last!

CONTEMPLATING THE NAVEL

October 1999

I go back to the days of the *Pittsburgh Press* when bellybuttons weren't allowed to be seen in pictures, even when we had a model wearing a two-piece bathing suit. Yes, we were on Mars. At least, young people today would certainly assume so.

An artist would "airbrush" the model's bellybutton. Erase it. By so doing, we allowed readers to assume we are hatched, not born attached to our mothers by an umbilical cord. Who talked about such things back then? For all we knew, we were hatched. It was easier that way.

Well, guess what. We've come down from Mars. We are in the middle of "midriff madness." Have you noticed?

Now, according to the recent fashion trends from observant analysts, the midriff, including our navel/bellybutton, is listed as a major focus of what's new and what we can expect to see more of.

Airbrushing disappeared decades ago. We bravely opted for harsh reality. Face it and move on, we said. But we weren't willing to go too far. We just avoided showing two-piece suits, except from the back.

Even the heroine in TV's *I Dream of Jeannie* couldn't show her bellybutton even though her midriff was bared in her harem outfit.

We were holding onto our dignity, after all.

If we'd known brushing off the airbrush might lead to today's trend toward "midriff madness," we might have fought to keep it. I for one would like to see it again, especially on designer's drawing boards.

It seems the new pants for spring of the new millennium (much like the pants of 1999) are waistless and low-rise, according to reports from Paris and New York. That means they hang on the hipbones. And that means an exposed navel. Jackets are shrunken in silhouettes and tops are gathered with drawstrings for a bellybutton revelation.

BB no longer signifies Bill Blass. His logo (granted, the B's were back to back) is no longer his own. BB means bellybutton. What else?

Camisoles and tanks are cropped too. Nothing is meant to be tucked in, even if you could. Crop it all off. Exposure. It's all about exposure.

Raise your arm to bid adieu to your toddler at the bus stop and you are going to show your bellybutton. Count on it. Raise your arm to ask a question in computer class and yes, southern-exposure.com. Raise your arm to squeeze the Charmin at the supermarket and you'll raise more than Mr. Whipple's eyebrows.

Now, granted, I am not worthy to bare mine. I don't want to, for one thing. But I can't help but wonder if I would if I were a tight and taut young thing. Or even a tight and taut old thing. What if I had a washboard tummy? I'm told the expression for perfection is now a "six-pack" middle. Whatever.

It isn't bad enough they want us to let it all hang out around the midsection. They want our arms and backs and shoulders to dare to be bare as well.

Show and tell takes on new meaning.

Okay, I know all these body-baring styles are really meant for the young shoppers of which I am no longer one and can't recall when I was.

Is there reason to find midriff madness, and the ultimate baring of the bellybutton, offensive, or should we just see it as another phase, here today and gone when we don't buy it?

HOPE IS THE ONLY OPTION

February 2001

Yesterday my son turned thirty. It's a milestone, but what year isn't? I believe that even more as I write today. While I have always been grateful for the privilege of being Drew's mother, I have had the good fortune to be here to watch him grow.

I never had to make use of a clause in my will that expressed my wishes as to who should raise him if something happened to me while he was young. When you are a single parent and a first-time mother at age forty-one, you give that decision a great deal of thought.

My parents could not have done it, and sadly, both were gone by the time Drew was eight. I chose Guy, the oldest of his three half-brothers and one half-sister, because he is a great example of a survivor, a man of principles, who is caring, hard-working, generous, and kind. He was like that even at twenty and today, at age forty-nine, moreso.

Where is this leading?

A little over a month ago, I was diagnosed with breast cancer. The joy of this writing on this particular day is that I have coped with the diagnosis, I have come through the segmental mastectomy, and I soon will begin the radiation treatments. I am moving forward with the reality of the disease millions of women already know firsthand, many with more radical surgeries than mine, who pick up their lives and keep going. I pray to be as brave.

I have told readers many details of my life over the past forty-five years. It is only natural I share this as well.

It came out of the blue, totally unexpected.

Saying or typing the words "breast cancer" does not come easily. I must be talking about somebody else. It cannot be me. But, of course, it can.

I have no idea how many women might be reading this today who recall vividly when someone looked at them and declared the feared words.

Your life changes that second. Nothing looks the same or feels the same. Not the air you are breathing, the hospital hallway you are carefully negotiating, the snow that falls on your hair and eyebrows as you head for your car.

The sky has always been there, and so have the people on the street, the buildings, the announcer on your car radio, the sound of horns honking, and a boombox carried by a young man waiting to cross the street.

Minutes ago, your world changed, and yet all that was there is still there. You just can't comprehend it. Let's face it. We take sounds and sights of everyday life for granted until tragedy strikes. Mine, at this stage, is not a tragedy. I am here, and I am optimistic.

Through the years, I have sympathized, empathized, cared about, cried for, suffered with, written to, consoled many friends diagnosed with serious illnesses, including breast cancer.

I was having my annual mammogram and, coincidentally, planned to visit with a dear friend who had a recurrence of her breast cancer. She was due to have more surgery that same day.

After my mammogram, I thought, I will sit with Jan. She has been through more than her share the past ten years.

I was assuming I would sail through the mammogram ritual.

The radiologist who informed me all was not good was to the point. Even without the eventual core biopsy to confirm what he considered "suspicious," he laid it on the line in no uncertain terms. "Get a surgeon," he said.

I followed my plan and sat with my friend and her mother. It was not the time to share my news. But I saw myself. I felt guilty for my selfishness. I was genuine in my concern for my friend, but now I was turning it around, seeing myself as the patient.

Telling my son was the hardest part.

I waited until after the biopsy was done the following week. I hadn't any information that would make it easier for him.

We were many miles apart when I told him, and that was frustrating for both of us.

Without elaborating, I can tell you I am not the same person I was. And, I suppose, neither is he, this thirtieth birthday. But I am here and so is he. That fact alone is to be celebrated.

Just as it happened to me unexpectedly, another woman is walking into a breast care center somewhere thinking about her new slipcovers or a lunch date. Then life changes.

"When I have hit bumps in the road," my son reminded me in a recent letter, "my mom always said to count my blessings and look at the glass as half full, not half empty. I know you are scared. Me too. But you'll be fine."

He tossed my words to him right back at me. It was powerful and what I needed from my only child. No, from the man my child has become.

My glass, this day, because I have him, and my friends, is not just half full. It is overflowing.

BACK TO THE PROM

August 2001

The invitation was too precious to ignore. I just had to get there. The invitation had come from my namesake, Barbara Michaels, who had invited those who meant something in her parents' lives to gather for a renewal of their wedding vows. Within a few days I had booked my flight to Baltimore, then to Salisbury, Maryland, about twenty miles from Ocean Pines, where Bill and Emily retired about nine years ago.

Retired? Both are probably busier now than ever. Why am I not surprised?

Emily ("Effie") Matheny was my best friend from grade school through junior and senior high and then college. We walked to school, home for lunch, then back to school and home again most days, missing very few as I recall, unless one of us had measles or chicken pox.

We lived near each other and traveled to each other's houses across back lawns and alleys several times each day. We spent all that time together and were no sooner in our respective homes than we were on the phone with each other. I have no idea what we had to say all that time, but we were joined at the hip, that's for sure.

Bill McIntire was always in the picture. Effie adored him. She would race up two flights of high school stairs just to be able to be coming down and pass him on the way to a class.

In Effie's old Character Book in which friends would write their thoughts—there was a sentence to be completed which began, "Happiness is...

Bill, at age thirteen, had completed it by writing "with Effie." It was 1943.

198

I didn't attend their wedding.

How could I have missed my best friend's wedding?

Well, I had gone to New York that fall of 1951, to pursue an acting career. I was starting a new job and couldn't come home for her wedding, which was December 27. Sad but true. So it seemed even more important that I be there to celebrate the marriage after fifty years, having missed it the first time around.

There are grandchildren—Spencer, Kyle, Holly and Mea—and they are a lively bunch and beautiful to behold. Add the five grown children of her only sister, and their broods, plus friends, and you have a party waiting to happen.

It happened. With all the joy you could imagine.

I sat back and observed most of my visit, although Effie and I babbled during a nice long day at the beach, just the two of us. Like old times.

Effie's sister, Jeanne, who was her matron of honor, had also married her high school sweetheart, a boy named Bill Irvin, who passed away three years ago. We remembered him fondly. Effie and I used to catch them kissing good night on her front porch.

We indulged in fresh corn, tomatoes, hamburgers, and cakes and pies nonstop for three days. Better than any four-star restaurant.

Love was all around—at the church the day of the ceremony and at the yacht club reception, where the DJ known as Hawaiian George even played Effie's late father's favorite song, "Down Mexico Way," and Frank Sinatra's "My Way."

Guests for the most part were mostly Sinatra-era fans, and we obliged by swooning.

Ed Sloan, the husband of their firstborn daughter, Janelle, thanked Effie and Bill for his wife of twenty years; their son, Jim, toasted his parents and thanked them for their inspiration; and Barbara thanked them for teaching how to love and their influence in her life.

Barbara had written a poem for her parents, which she asked me to read at the church because she knew she would cry.

Not a dry eye at that point. Mine certainly weren't. It was touching.

At the reception, Bill tried to make a brief speech as a granddaughter clutched his leg, but he, too, was teary. Good tears. And a few sad ones.

Bill is a prostate cancer survivor, and he walked me through my own cancer diagnosis a few weeks after his treatments ended. It's yet another bond. And we are doing well.

Before the renewal of vows at the church, family photos were shown on a large screen, and my eyes filled with tears when I saw many in which the three of us beamed for the Brownie lens at ages fifteen, some in my backyard.

We saw the 1951 bill from their wedding night at Hotel Schenley in Pittsburgh. It totaled $13. Breakfast in bed cost more than the room, but going to the Plaza would not have been any more memorable for these twenty-one-year-olds who seem to have loved each other forever.

As they danced together fifty years later, I saw two teenagers at the prom, gazing into each other's eyes, as if time stood still.

It's love as you expect it to be when you are young. Or, in this case, as you grow older.

A PERFECT DAY IN JUNE

September 2002

We all have entered this ninth month of 2002 with never-to-be-forgotten memories of the day we changed just one year ago.

Tributes are justified when showing us the courage exhibited by the families directly affected by 9/11. Could I do it? I'm not so sure.

The recent Diane Sawyer television special with sixty-three babies—never to know their fathers—born to widows since that date had me weeping for their loss, then smiling at the babies' innocence and the hope they inspire.

My own memory was jarred this week as I was cleaning out papers and various notebooks kept far too long.

A small connection, but there it was.

I had a small, narrow, loose-leaf-style notebook in my hand, ready to toss. I hesitated when I saw New York scribbled on the front, and the date, June 2001.

More specifically, I had been in Battery Park, near the World Trade Center, and as soon as I realized the connection, I slid down to the floor and began to read some of the scribblings: "yachts, rollerbladers, sunbathers, lovers, eaters. Many dogs."

Insignificant. No hint of horror. Rather boring.

Is that what I saw? Pure joy? Pure happiness?

Yes. That's what I saw. No story in that, but I took notes just the same.

Life was good. I watched dog walkers with six or more furry creatures on one lead pulling toward the green grass. I had lunch on a restaurant patio, overlooking the harbor.

I made a note: "Hear dog walkers get paid well. Might be a

profession to consider." My mood was light.

I was just observing as life, Battery Park-style, passed me by.

This was a piece of heaven in the middle of skyscrapers and financial ups and downs. Even dogs found it worth a woof or two of appreciation.

Trees and grass. What could be better?

My notes continued: "Park is like an oasis; fuels the soul of New Yorkers and tourists alike."

Note: "World Trade Center. It is surrounded by shops, a dry cleaner, a veterinarian's office, 24-hour grocery store. Well-patrolled, great place to live."

On another page: "Flowers! WTC has underground mall; day-care workers stroll with toddlers attached by strings of rope."

A disheveled woman, her arms in the air, is shouting "America" at the top of her lungs. I jotted that down.

Now that woman seems prophetic. At the time, she registered in my mind as a bag lady with delusions. Color material, in case I write a column.

There was no fear this day, only happiness. It was an ordinary day with no frills.

My notes were brief. A column did not seem likely. At the J. Crew store in the WTC mall, I duly noted a purchase: "Gift for me, black sweater, $68."

Selfish. Not for a column.

These were hasty notes done as I walked on what was to become hallowed ground within three months.

I was noting my impressions, my joy, my good fortune being there so soon after breast-cancer treatment, feeling absolutely on top of the world, grateful for friends, grateful for life. Grateful for Orso's pizza and friend Tom Julian.

Average stuff suddenly seems awesome. Especially in New York.

How could anyone smelling the flowers, feeling the sun, buying a sweater, posing for pictures, imagine what was coming?

A dozen or so years earlier, a photographer and I did a fashion shoot for the *Pittsburgh Press*, using much of the scenic background, the benches, the street lamps, the wall bordering the harbor beyond the WTC, the Statue of Liberty in the distance.

I also found the magazine featuring those photos as I went through my boxes of accumulated stuff from fifty years. It's another reminder of what was before 9/11.

As I roamed "Shadyside ... the Art Festival of Walnut Street" last month, I was aware that photographs or paintings of the Twin Towers were in great supply.

And while I know through technology they were eliminated from the skyline in many movies set in New York City before 9/11, every once in awhile a movie comes on television that has not erased the towers. And, for just a moment, I am transported back to that summer day in June under their shadow.

But then I'm brought back to today, to reality.

I don't think I need my notes or pictures to remember the tragedy. I won't forget.

But I do need to be reminded to appreciate a happy day when it comes along. There are no guarantees there will be another.

So, I will keep my notes.

DIRT IS NOT A DIRTY WORD

July 2003

This time last year, few of us had heard of Quecreek. We weren't even sure how to spell it or pronounce it.

But since last July 25, we have learned.

Amid lingering questions about blame, settlements, and mine safety, uppermost in our thoughts is the rescue—nine men trapped and then miraculously saved in the Somerset County mine.

I think about it because this is the time of the year I usually head for Stone Harbor, New Jersey.

Last year, as the ordeal entered into its second day and we were watching the rescue efforts on television, I was on the road, heading for the beach. I remember driving close to Somerset on the turnpike and slowing down as I approached the area where the attempt to rescue men sandwiched between rock and water was taking place.

I don't know what I expected to see. Of course, I saw nothing.

Here I was, traveling toward a destination where I would have peace and sunshine, peaches and fresh corn, no worries. I would soon be in water neck-high. Somewhere off the highway in a quiet hamlet, nine men were buried underground. The likely outcome, it seemed then, was not good.

I reached my destination six hours later. I spent the greater part of the next twenty-four hours not relaxing on the beach but watching the rescue attempts and the aftermath on television. I managed to stay up to watch all nine miners brought to safety.

After each rescue, I thought I would go to bed. It was after midnight. I couldn't.

I thought of my brief history with mines. Part of that history is being born and raised in coal-mining country. I felt I knew these families who sent their men into the dark and damp and dreary underground each day.

I was born and raised in Uniontown, where my father began his medical practice as physician for the Frick Mine in nearby Revere.

I envisioned the faces of the Quecreek miners as being much like the miners who would fill the main street of Uniontown on Saturdays, as well as those I knew personally because of my father. I could see Joe Boskovitch. I remember Andy Urban. I remember Teddy Skomra.

I often went on house calls with "Doc." I would go to his office after school, and he would take me on his rounds. More often than not, we went to row houses in what were referred to as "coal patches," on the outskirts of town. Union Supply Company stores were close by.

I can remember the men who had just gotten home from their shifts, their weathered faces still black with soot. The dirt on their hands never seemed to be completely removed from their fingernails, not even with lye soap.

The memory is so strong, as is the smell of a pot of soup beans on the stove and fresh bread. I never knew the hardships or the danger of mining and what these miners endured to make a living.

Seeing dirt under a man's fingernails and in the pores of his skin was to see courage.

WE FEEL THE LOSS

November 2003

Suddenly you feel a part of history. You leave your office and enter a restaurant, order your lunch, and talk about important things, such as your plans for the weekend, a new dress, the quality of your salad and its puny serving of lettuce. And then you go to pay your check, and the words you are hearing from the woman in front of you don't make sense.

"The president...shot...seriously...it just happened."

You wonder how such rumors get started. By the time you reach the street, you know it's more than rumor.

You have heard the words that will live with you the rest of your life. And you wonder what will happen, all the time refusing to believe what you have just heard is fact.

You hurry past people on the street, wondering how they can be so carefree and how they can laugh and joke with one another.

Your knees are shaking and you feel a coldness come over your body as you enter the newsroom of the newspaper office where you work.

And you know it has happened.

President John F. Kennedy, who just a few days ago was pictured with his young son John-John peering from beneath the Chief Executive's desk, all smiles, is dead.

There are tears, and they flow freely as you grip your stomach and try to grasp the meaning of what has happened.

You wonder if there is any hope for the world or for people who could do such a thing. You mix thoughts of the Kennedy family, the vibrant youth of his wife who was a witness to the sheer horror of an assassin's aim which hit its mark.

Just why you sit down and feel compelled to put your

thoughts on paper escapes you.

It seems the only way to make it believable.

Millions of Americans have experienced this today. I am only one of them.

*****

I wrote the above column the day President Kennedy was assassinated. It was a Friday, November 22, 1963. It appeared in the *Pittsburgh Press* Saturday, November 23—forty years ago to this very date.

Writing seemed the best way to capture a few hours which, of course, would drag into days of watching television as the drama unfolded. Suspect Lee Harvey Oswald was caught and then himself shot by Jack Ruby. Then followed the funeral November 25, the riderless horse, boots reversed in their stirrups, young John's salute, Jacqueline's face behind the black veil, muffled drum rolls.

I sobbed the entire time it took to put my words on paper that day. I cried whenever I looked at the picture of President Kennedy at his desk, mischievous John-John at his feet.

When grown-up John Jr. died in a plane crash in 1999, I thought of that day again, and that famous picture, when what the future held for both father and son was yet to be realized.

I had been captivated by Camelot. I freely admit that. Nothing bad was supposed to happen in what seemed like a fairy tale.

Clear as the day itself was the image I observed as I walked toward the *Press* building that fall afternoon in 1963, half walking, half running across Equitable Plaza, wanting to get the facts coming fast and furious over teletype machines.

In those days the machines were lined up inside the left front windows of the second floor of what is now the *Post-Gazette*, facing the Boulevard of the Allies.

National and international news spewed from those machines

and created a constant humming/typing sound in newspaper offices, a sound, along with the pounding of typewriters, now gone as new technology has been realized.

I looked up as I crossed the Boulevard of the Allies and saw everyone hovering over the machines, pulling the papers off as fast as they were printing.

Years later, happier years, my desk at the *Press* would be at those windows where the teletypes once whirred and whistled.

The president had not been pronounced dead at that time. There was still hope, and before I sat down to write the column, I was sure he would not die. But this fairy tale did not have a happy ending. His death came within the hour, about 2:30 p.m.

And I began to type.

Sadly, forty years later, it seems we still don't know the whole story. We do recall the shock, the sadness, the fear, and the sense of loss unlike anything we had known. That remains true—and very real.

REMEMBERING MAMAS

May 2004

Talk about a play I loved, and a role I loved to play, John VanDruten's *I Remember Mama* is front and center.

I still remember most of Marta Hansen's lines, having performed in the play at Westminster College as a sophomore and again as a junior when I was just eighteen…and then, some thirty-five years later, I was Mama again at Robert Morris Colonial Theater.

I had, in the interim, become a Mama for real. My son was old enough to rehearse lines with me for that performance. He was in the audience opening night, and he reminded me I had left out a line in Act II.

In 1948 at Westminster, I met Mady Christians, the actress who played Mama on Broadway (Marlon Brando was sixteen-year-old Nels), when she was a guest lecturer. It was Miss Christians who told me then I was too tall to ever become a leading lady in the theater.

Years later I saw Liv Ullmann, the Norwegian actress, portray Mama in a 1979 Broadway revival which I didn't like at all. A favorite actress, Irene Dunne, was in the movie version.

Yet another Mama, Peggy Wood, came to the Pittsburgh Nixon Theater in *Girls in 509*, and we talked about her eight years on television in the *I Remember Mama* series.

Little Lake Theater has the play on its summer schedule. So many Mamas are on my mind.

Remembering Mama—or Mom, Mother, Mumsie, or any other favorite name—is what we are doing today. We who no longer have our mothers with us have our special memories.

The truth is, they are always with us.

Little things remind us.

Those special little things they said or did are never gone. And in some instances, we become our mothers. We might resemble them but even more than that, we do similar things, or we are seldom without their influence, one way or the other.

Leslie Wohlfarth's mother, Lahela Samuels Mulvihill, was one hundred years old when she died in 1998. Until her final illness she never spent a day in the hospital except to give birth to Leslie and her brother, Mead.

"What I remember so well about Mumsie (a name given by Leslie's first husband, the late Don Brockett) was the way her closet always had a faint scent of Joy, her favorite perfume. As a little girl I would open that door just to breathe in the lovely scent, wishing for the day I would be old enough to wear perfume.

"I also remember she would often take me on her antiquing jaunts, and I am sure she was responsible for my love of all things old and beautiful."

When Dolores Zegarelli thinks of her late mother, Rose Rainey, she thinks of her sayings, her enjoyment of dancing, and her positive outlook in finding the good in people.

"When I would get upset or angry, she always told me, 'Life is too short. Forgive and forget.' I try to do that.

"There are still times I will say to myself, How would you handle this, Mom? I still think of her as being a part of my life."

Mrs. Rainey was seventy-nine when she was hit by a bus in Hallendale, Florida, and died as a result of her injuries. She was on her way to a store to buy Easter candy.

How she would have loved seeing her first great-grandchild, born three months ago, and named Bria Rose Zegarelli.

Eleanor Schano Feeney's mother, also named Eleanor, died just a few months ago at age ninety-eight.

"When I was about ten, my mother and I took a bus to Downtown to shop for clothes and I remember I always had to wear my patent-leather shoes and white gloves. Mom explained that a lady always wore white gloves when going to town.

"When Mom held my gloved hand, I felt love, warmth, and security that surrounds me today."

Terri Tobay's mother, Isabel Boskovitch, died in Uniontown at the age of eighty-one. "She was hard-working and had a sensitivity to people's needs. She faced many obstacles but was full of laughter and, most of all, full of love," recalls Terri.

If we have been fortunate enough to know the love and sacrifices of a good mother, we are blessed. But it isn't always their devotion to us or their sacrifices that linger.

"Oh, banana oil," my mother would mutter when she couldn't get the lid off a jar or she had some other frustration.

To this day, I don't know where that expression came from. I never asked. But I remember it, and it makes me smile.

She wore a fragrance called After Five, and also loved Worth's Je Reviens. Her fingers were swollen with arthritis, somewhat like mine are now, but when she stroked my hair, I was always soothed.

Today, as we remember Mama, even if we are mothers ourselves, we are once again the child. And that's a good thing.

COMING FULL CIRCLE

December 2004

Life sometimes comes full circle.

That's how I felt recently when Liza McDonald visited me during a trip to the East Coast from her home in Los Angeles, where she is a film editor.

On a whim she had decided to rent a car when she got to Chicago and hit a few cities in Ohio, West Virginia, Massachusetts, Iowa, and Pennsylvania, where she had friends she hadn't seen in a while. I would be the Pennsylvania stop-over.

That's quite an undertaking. Soon after she returned to the West Coast, she found herself on the road again, this time headed to Las Vegas for the funeral of dancer/comedian Peggy Ryan, 80, who died earlier this month and who had married Liza's father, the late Ray McDonald, in the late '40s.

Our connection, if you can call it that, actually goes back to 1951.

In fact, during her visit, as we sat in my living room, all cozy in our jammies and robes watching the PBS series *Broadway: The American Musical,* I was remembering how it all began.

When I went to New York to pursue acting (I never pursued it as much as I dreamed of it), I rented a room from a woman in a Third Avenue building. The woman, Jessie Fraser Jonker, was Liza's grandmother.

Liza, then a toddler, lived in California with her sister, Meg, and their mother, Elisabeth Fraser, Jessie's daughter, an actress.

Who would have thought one day I would be sitting in my living room, eating chocolate chip ice cream with the daughter of a woman I had admired in movies and who was also the granddaughter of a woman I lived with when I was all of twenty-two?

Mrs. Jonker worked as a telephone operator at the Belmont Plaza Hotel, and she often talked about her daughter and grandchildren in California. But I never met them.

So, fifty-three years later…

We watched the PBS series the two nights she was here with more than mere interest in theater.

We were both hoping Moss Hart's wartime play, *Winged Victory*, would be mentioned in the early segments dealing with Broadway in the '40s and, better yet, we might even see her parents, who had been in that show. That didn't happen.

Liza had first gotten in touch with me several years ago when she read a column on the Internet in which I mentioned her mother and grandmother. We've corresponded ever since.

The first of the two-night PBS series dealt with vaudeville as the predecessor of the Broadway musicals that were to come. Liza also was hoping there might be a clip in which her father, Ray, then sixteen, and his sister Grace, nineteen, would appear. They were a brother-sister dance team who started in vaudeville.

That didn't happen either.

Ray McDonald was one of the Air Force servicemen who made up the bulk of the cast of *Winged Victory*, and it was when he met Liza's mother, Elisabeth, also in the cast. They married in 1944 but were divorced by the time I went to New York in 1951. He had by then married Peggy Ryan, with whom he appeared in several films. Both were dancers.

Liza takes great pride in her father's musical talents. We played a tape she had of him dancing with his sister when they were in their teens. Her eyes lit up. "That's my father," she said. "Look at that smile." We both watched with smiles on our faces as well.

The day before Liza was to arrive, TCM was airing the 1947 film *Good News*, in which her father had a featured role with June Allyson. It was his last movie for MGM, but he later appeared with Ryan in *Shamrock Hill* and *All Ashore*.

I lived at the movies in those days. I remembered McDonald very well (*Life Begins for Andy Hardy*, 1941) and Liza's mother as well from *All My Sons* and *Young at Heart* with Doris Day and Frank Sinatra. They both appeared in the film version of *Winged Victory*, released in 1944 after the theater tour.

In a biography of the actor/dancer on the Web site www.classicimages.com, it states that his career went into a decline in the '50s and, in 1959, he took his own life at the age of thirty-eight with an overdose of sleeping pills.

To which Liza retorts, absolutely not true. "My father did not die of an overdose of sleeping pills, a lingering rumor which is, happily, not true. He was in a hotel room after appearing on *The Ed Sullivan Show* and unfortunately choked on food and died, in the same manner as Tommy Dorsey. The medical examiner confirmed he had died of avisceral congestion, or choking on food. New York papers printed retractions after rumors of a suicide leaked, but the original story has survived."

In darkened movie theaters, when I was about twelve, I saw Liza's father in his prime. In my teens I saw both her parents on stage in *Winged Victory* and in several movies. Liza had not yet been born. I was thinking about this as we had second helpings of ice cream. Our connection had come full circle.

"*I prefer the classics. I'm built for them. I have a big nose and a big voice. I like being part of greatness. I have always wanted to play Peter Pan, but it's obvious I never will.*"

—Dame Judith Anderson, 1962

"*I wouldn't give any of my children even a gentle push toward show business, but if they decided that's what they wanted, I'd do anything in the world to help.*"

—Phyllis Diller, 1960

"*I can't say what road my career would have taken if I hadn't won the title of Miss America. I entered because I needed money to continue studying music.*"

—Bess Myerson, 1963

"*As soon as my foot is in the light onstage, I am home. It is what I love to do. It is what I have always loved to do.*"

—Polly Bergen, 2001

"*I don't like to be away from home and children. I hope to marry again eventually, but I'm not looking right now.*"

—Debbie Reynolds, 1959

my family

doctors

nostalgia

my child

grace

nostalgia

love

great friends

friends

nostalgia

passion

my pets

my sister

parents

faith

babies

my path

Why

grandchild

love

home

talent

THE COMFORT
OF A WET NOSE

October 1982

As we read of the horrors of war, of massacres, senseless shootings, holocausts, suffering of the elderly, children waiting for transplants, how can the loss of one cocker spaniel cause so much pain? Don't reason with me today. There is an aching. There is a loneliness.

In the thirty years I have worked as a reporter I have found myself writing about the loss of another pet named Mitzi, and then later, the acquisition of a new family member, another blond cocker, named Stormy.

I bought Stormy to ease the pain of losing Mitzi. He lived with my parents, as did Mitzi, and was their companion for eleven years. And then he, too, was gone. Neither ever lived with me as I had left for college and later had my own apartment in Pittsburgh.

But while each lived a fairly long life, although too short by human standards, and I returned home often, neither dog was truly mine. Soot was mine, from the moment I held him in the palm of my hand as a puppy until the dreadful moment I handed him to my vet to be put to rest some thirteen years later.

We get pretty sappy about our pets. I wish it helped knowing others have gone through this. It doesn't.

Since I acquired Soot, in the last few years, 1975 and 1979, I have lost both my parents. I cried long and hard at their passing because life would never be the same again and I knew that. But we go on.

But you see, always there to comfort me was Soot. A furry head nestled in your lap when you are low does far more tranquilizing than any little white pill. If you have had a pet, either a cat or a dog and even a bird or a hamster, you know the incredible closeness which develops, even without your realizing it. I have sat and poured out my heart to all of my pooches during my years of growing pains…when mother scolded or a best beau went off to war. Or I agonized over a lost love, a punishment, an argument with a friend.

The warmth of that body next to you is security for both of you. The wet nose is a source of comfort. It is little wonder taking animals into nursing homes has met with such success. The feeling of love and caring needs no words. And that is the joy, but also the sorrow when the quiet caring is gone.

When I decided to have a pet of my own, I asked the kennel owner to meet me in a parking lot near Donaldson's Crossroads with one black male puppy. Not having to pick one from a litter made it easier. I knew what I wanted. At the time I needed him more than he needed me. I needed the responsibility, the companionship, the love. I was adrift in my personal life.

For thirteen years he was a joy. During personally traumatic times he was my therapy. He saved my sanity, giving me something to think about other than my own woes and he was my dearest friend for two years before my son was born. Then our lives changed and he was now the family pet, no longer just mine. Now he had a family beyond his working mistress who had to leave him alone each day.

I made up for it in the evenings when we headed for his runs in the park, but the days must have seemed very long when I was gone. I still have a mattress he chewed through to the springs, and there are puppy teeth marks on the wooden arms of a rocking chair. But the negatives were few.

When I left for the hospital the morning my son was born in 1971, I looked back at Soot, his head cocked as if wondering why

I was leaving him again at two o'clock in the morning. A new routine was about to begin. I said to him as I closed the door behind me, "Dear Soot, you will never be alone again."

Silly you say? Perhaps. But his life was going to change with the new family member, and our beloved sitter, Nancy, arriving each day for the next eleven years. He was always gentle with my son as an infant and the day I interviewed Nancy for the job, even before she saw the baby who would become like her own, he jumped into her lap and they were friends immediately.

So, I had to make the decision I never wanted to make last week and after sharing my life for thirteen years and my son's life for eleven years, our Soot was relieved of his pain and put to sleep. I had hoped and prayed he would simply pass away quietly in his sleep. He had not been well. It was time.

I have been in the vet's office often and watched others leave with empty blankets and I have felt sorrow for them, but selfishly I was always thankful it wasn't me. My father was a medical doctor who served in the South Pacific and he saw death in every form. But he, too, cried each time we lost a pet. He was not ashamed, neither am I.

I see Soot in every corner of the house and it has only been a week. He is not curled on my bed and I miss that loving lick each morning when I awoke. Special dog food for a "condition" and all kinds of drops for an eye problem, plus digitoxin for his heart…still he survived and wagged his tail and lavished us with his attention, right to the end.

He leaves not just us as humans, but also his buddy, Beau. Yes, I have another dog, a springer spaniel I acquired when Soot was about four. He really has become my son's playmate as Soot began to age. I think I was preparing myself for the day I would lose Soot, but Beau, too, needed a home or he might have been put down.

He has some physical "imperfections," but he is family too.

I still have dear Beau and it is good to have a water dish on the kitchen floor and to have dog food on the shopping list. It helps, but it doesn't take away the pain.

One does not replace the other. We are all missing Soot.

IT'S ALL GOING TOO FAST

May 1989

It's over. Well, all but the shouting.

Through the years readers have been patient as I have shared my son's adventures. Locking me out of the house when he was two, his basement plays, the tooth lost in the snow (and we found it), the first sleepover party, the reality of Santa Claus, our getting-to-know-you vacation in Florida.

Drew is eighteen. Suddenly. He graduates from Taylor-Allderdice High School Wednesday.

In the last year or two I have wanted to slow him down, stop him literally in his tracks, and say, "Hey, wait a minute. Let me look at you. Let me just stand here and look at you. It's all going too fast."

It's universal among parents, I'm sure, but there is a special feeling when you raise a child by yourself, and it was just Drew and me from the day he was born.

I learned to put a sandbox together, to assemble a Hot Wheels bike, and to tie a necktie.

It is double work. Double worry. But it also is double joy. Women who raise sons alone work, pay the mortgage, actually know where the fuse box is located, balance the checkbook, shop, do the laundry, cook, taxi, buy the Christmas tree, decorate the Christmas tree, get rid of the Christmas tree—and discipline when needed. Discipline in the voice and action. Softness in the touch.

I have never grounded Drew. I never had the occasion. I smacked his behind once. The red imprint of my hand frightened me. I never did it again.

Because there has been just me, this son of mine has enriched my life in a way I cannot compare to two-parent households. It isn't what I have done for him. It is what he has done for me.

For eighteen years he has been part of my daily plan. Whether I was making his school lunch, helping with his Willie Stargell speech for a fourth-grade assembly, picking him up at midnight at Reizenstein Middle School after a ski trip, or watching him at swim classes at the Salvation Army during my lunch hour.

Many parents wanted Little League to be over. I wished it were just beginning. I remember when his Little League coach told me I should buy him an athletic cup. Me? What is that? But I did it.

"What size?" asked the salesman.

Drew was only eight. "Small," I whispered.

I could never find the mercury when I took his temperature. I went by the touch. The high temperatures that terrified me in the middle of the night, and then in the morning, the exhilaration when he was cool—and hungry.

When he was ten and I drove past a girl he knew, they would stick out their tongues at each other. Now he drives the car and they wink at each other.

Having a son got me to an honest-to-goodness wrestling match and taught me who Jimmy Snuka was. Football, baseball, basketball are familiar to me now. I know Magic Johnson is great. I know Mark Malone wasn't. And I know Michael Jordan's basketball number is 23. That's why Drew chose it for his years of high school baseball. Just last week I washed that uniform for the last time.

Peanut butter and jelly sandwiches fade and give way to salsa and ribs. So do requests for miniature cars, action figures, and hand-held electronic games.

His is a typical boy's room. Never clean. Walls covered with posters, lots of bottles of cologne, his own phone, a miniature basketball hoop over the closet door. Under the bed, a girlie magazine. I found it. I looked at it. I put it back.

My living room floor is going to look different when he heads for college. It won't have four pairs of basketball shoes as an obstacle course.

I love this boy. He is my reason for all that I do. I cannot imagine the years that preceded his arrival in my world.

I didn't make it this far alone. Dear friends helped: his "adopted aunts" with whom we have shared Christmas for seventeen years. And Nancy, my irreplaceable sitter and friend. Dr. Bill, the pediatrician who never sent a bill.

What brings tears is that much of what we have done this past year was for the last time as he prepares to move on to college. I have loved his friends—Jon, Tat, Nima, Jesse, Charley—some of whom slept in that pile of bodies in our living room—and I want to know what they do with their lives as well.

Memories. My mother was buried the day he had his fourth birthday party. When he was five, I lost him at the beach for fifteen minutes—I died a thousand times. When he was eight, he said a final goodbye to his only grandpa. He had chicken pox at fourteen. Pneumonia in one lung at fifteen. We bought Stridex complexion pads when he was sixteen. And the clock keeps ticking.

There are more good things ahead. But they are the things Drew and I will share on an adult level. We are mother and son, but we haven't been mother and child for some time.

When did he start adding shaving cream to the shopping list? I barely noticed. I'll notice when I see him in his cap and gown Wednesday.

And I'm going to say to him, "Hey, slow down. Let me look at you. Let me just stand here and look at you."

FAITH AND FRIENDSHIP

December 1989

Christmas makes me think of my childhood friend Harriet.

I am fortunate to have had many friends of the Jewish faith, although I am not Jewish.

I was raised in a small town where proud ethnic names ending with "vich" or "ski" were more common. I was immersed and christened a Baptist when I was twelve. I thought I would drown because my minister had but one arm. He was strong. I survived.

When you are young, who knows the origin of a name, or whether the girl or boy you sit next to in arithmetic is Jewish, or Polish, or Baptist? It never mattered.

And I never thought much about Harriet Berkman's faith, except I remember going to a "celebration" for her and I wore shiny shoes and white anklets. I just never thought about a bat mitzvah meaning we were different. We grew up in the same neighborhood, sipped vanilla Cokes, played with our paper dolls, and went to the movies. What else mattered?

I remember the smells in her house, because her mother always had soup or cabbage on the stove. I remember her older brother Seymour used to tease us. I remember the gate at the top of the walkway to her house on Clarendon Avenue and how I would fly through it on my way to spend an afternoon playing. I think of her at Christmas because I remember a party I had. We were fifteen.

She disappeared for some time and I found her in the bathroom crying. She was very smart, and she wore thick glasses because her eyes were bad. I suppose she wasn't cool. She didn't date. She was simply the brightest girl in our class. And dear to me.

But she was crying because nobody had asked her to dance. It had nothing to do with her being Jewish, but, you see, she wasn't pretty. She was kind. She was funny. She was caring. But she wore thick glasses. I can still see her sitting on the edge of the tub holding those glasses, wiping her eyes and feeling miserable. I tried to console her, but I didn't know how. You can't brush that kind of pain away easily.

As the years passed, she and I kind of drifted apart. She went on and became a nurse in New York, married, and was happy, as far as I know. I would see her at high school reunions. She was attractive and she laughed a lot. And men asked her to dance.

Last week I was addressing Christmas cards. In my address book her name is crossed off, the address pale and faded. It has been so for many years as we lost touch, but seeing the name always triggers memories of growing up.

At our fortieth high school class reunion, I presented the memorial to classmates who had died since we graduated.

Harriet Berkman Starr. All of the names on the list meant something to me, but reading hers caused my throat to catch—because I didn't know she had died. She mattered in my life. And yet, I didn't know.

If I could give a single gift this holiday, it would be the gift of friendship. Like mine and Harriet's, brief as it was. It should never be taken for granted. I would wrap that gift with a bow the size of the world.

That's what Christmas does. It reminds us of such things. German, Russian, Catholic, Protestant, or Jew. We need to be reminded.

Reach out this holiday, and forget color, religion, social status—and thick glasses. We can't avoid the pain of growing up. But we can learn from it and be good to each other.

LOSING PART OF YOURSELF

June 1998

It is indeed ironic that my column of last week had me filled with memories of traveling Route 51. I had started the column weeks ago, but began to dwell on it more and more since the middle of May. I was traveling the route almost daily, between my Pittsburgh home and Uniontown, because my sister was very ill.

Columnists open their hearts and souls to readers. To do otherwise would, it seems to me, be pretending. Although baring private thoughts in print can be painful, I must do that today as I say farewell to my beautiful sister, B.J. She passed away, not quietly as I had hoped, but slipping hour by hour from early morning until the evening of June 10.

We know death is part of the living we are blessed with day to day. But I doubt we are ever prepared for that moment, whether or not the death is expected. I was prepared, I thought. For weeks I would end my visits by going to her house and looking at pictures, touching her possessions, many of them in our home when we were growing up. I knew she would not be coming there again, and yet I had not really believed it.

I dragged her deck furniture from the basement and noted that I must see about new cushions. I scrubbed kitchen cupboards and washed clothes. I threw out contents of those cupboards that had gathered dust. My sister had not been well for some time, but she never allowed me to do what I was now doing.

I dabbed her favorite perfume behind my ears. I took it to the hospital and touched her wrists with the moist Ombre Rose. I was preparing for her homecoming. I couldn't stop.

I honored her wishes, but I ached inside. I was losing her. This beautiful, talented, vivacious woman, two years and two weeks older than I, and someone I had shared so much with during the years prior to World War II, now began to withdraw from life.

When we were young, our names were often said in tandem: Bobbie and B. J. We double-dated often, shared a bedroom until she married, always had Halloween birthday party themes because we were both born in October, went to the hospital together to have our tonsils removed, and fought only over who would get to wear the new sweater for a dance at the teen club.

Some things might be better left unsaid, but when you have loved someone all your life and they are suddenly gone, it is all you can think about or talk about. To eat or read or watch television, even to laugh, suddenly seems wrong.

Perhaps that is why I kept scrubbing.

I am reminded, however, life goes on. Nowhere was that more evident than at the Cherry Tree Nursing Center, where she was cared for the last week of her life. Even as she went through what the nurses called "the dying process," which I had prayed she would not have to endure, I watched nurses and aides scurry past us, tending to those who were still drawing breath, many in a place only their own minds could comprehend.

You don't want someone you love to live like that, but when they start to leave you, you begin to want only to have them look at you and you want to feel warmth as their fingers are wrapped around yours. In reality, you know you must let go. You want her to let go as well, to end the pain in her heart and her frail body.

She had suffered two strokes, could not speak, swallow, or move her left side. A third stroke was diagnosed the day she passed away as she developed a high fever.

I wrapped my tanned fingers around her long, slender, and very pale fingers, which she always kept so perfectly manicured and painted with a lovely color. My hands are nothing like hers. I would study her almost perfect nose. Mine is nothing like hers. She wore glasses, usually very large and stylish ones, since we were in high school, and seeing her these past weeks without them I began to see her large brown eyes for the first time. But they were sad and in pain, and I felt much relieved when she closed them to nap.

Our family was small. There were just my parents and their two girls. Our parents died years ago, first my mother when my son, Drew, was four, and my father when Drew was just eight. He had his Aunt B.J. and his mom.

But more important, I had B.J. I needed her. Drew would know her, but not as I did. A young man can never know the nights of two giddy sisters sitting up and talking about boyfriends and our dreams, trying makeup, learning to ride a bike or roller-skate, listening to Stan Kenton, packing for Girl Scouts camp. We did just about everything together.

Life takes us in different directions at times, although B.J. was the first of us to enter a newspaper office as an employee. I followed her reluctantly, because my eyes had been set on Broadway.

And here I am, almost where she led me without realizing it.

During my travels on my infamous Route 51, I recalled so many things, not the least of which was to realize that my reason for continuing such excursions was no longer there.

I felt I had no anchor to what I always had considered my home, no reason to be passing that way again in any true meaningful sense—to pull up in front of her house, honk the horn, and see her beautiful and smiling face at the doorway.

It had not been smiling for such a long time. Part of me is gone, but I live the rest of my life for the two of us, in tandem, as in the beginning.

A PLEA TO PHYSICIANS

February 1999

When more than one person remarks that you seem a bit down, you probably are. We think we can hide feelings, but when you write a weekly column, it often creeps in. No hiding.

Well, yes, I have been sad. I appreciate the concern. As a columnist I sit down and write what I am feeling. I can't always be glad; I can't always be sad. Often I am mad. Two articles I read recently hit me where I live. At least where I have lived in past months.

I have been in a sad place since my only sister died. Natural sadness is prolonged because I am also mad. She passed away last June, but emptying her house, selling it, wrapping up loose ends, getting through a first holiday season without her have kept my emotions on a seesaw.

Unlike clowns who put on a happy face even when they are blue, columnists tend to bare all as fingers fly over computer keys and the thoughts transfer to the screen in printed words.

To lose B. J. has its own distinct pain. We all lose people we love. I've lost my parents and favorite relatives, an early love when he was just twenty, many friends and several pets, which we know become family. We love them, too. We survive somehow. We also change.

So, why am I still mad?

One reason was clearly identified in a personal reflection by Dr. Paul A. Carson, who practices internal medicine in the North Hills. It appeared in the *Post-Gazette.* He said losing his mother made him rethink his role as a doctor.

Because he is a doctor, his discovery, at least to me, was even more dramatic. And it hit home.

He and his family were disquieted after his mother's death because of the lack of communication between medical professionals and his family. She had the best medical care possible heading into surgery. That wasn't it.

No condolence. No phone call, no explanation of the sad outcome of her surgery from her doctors. Silence. That was the disquieting note. The patient dies. Deal with it. The doctor's role ends.

When my mother had surgery for a brain tumor almost twenty-four years ago, the surgeon never met with my father, my sister, or me. He never came to us in the waiting room after the surgery. He never called. I don't even know what he looked like, although I have never forgotten his name.

More recently, while I grieved and fought the terrible responsibility of carrying out my sister's living will, especially her final hours when we knew she would not make it through the day, I never heard from her doctor. Not that day. Nor since.

Should those left to grieve expect some act of compassion from a doctor?

A neurological report, especially a very bad prognosis, left on an answering machine is no way to communicate the news that the patient will probably die.

I had a similar experience at another hospital and with other doctors, when my sister was being treated almost two years ago. I begged for meetings with them and was promised we would, of course, all sit down and discuss the prognosis. She was discharged after two weeks. There was no meeting.

I should have ranted and raved. I was too sad to do so.

I should not have needed to rant and rave.

Now, months later, I seem to be ranting. I can't help it.

The other article I took to heart, written by Diana Block, dealt with the dilemma we face carrying out a loved one's living will. It's not an easy thing, especially if you must do it alone. It never leaves your mind.

I have a living will. It seems so easy to sit down with a lawyer and put down all the right words. But for the person left to interpret the words, it can be agonizing. And it was for me.

So, yes, sadness has been lingering, and it creeps in from time to time. It will get better. It has. Life goes on.

I don't want to criticize a profession that allows for medical miracles a small-town doctor like my late father would only have dreamed of fifty years ago.

But how about this miracle? What about transplants of compassion to those physicians whose hearts are sadly lacking? There's no technology involved. No "procedure." They wouldn't even need a donor. Just a change of heart.

LETTERS LEAVE A LEGACY

December 2002

How rare a personal letter will be in years to come. In fact, it is rare today. More's the pity. Many of us have succumbed to e-mail, myself included, although I still try to write my fair share of notes and letters by hand, because I know how much receiving such a note means to me.

Although I appreciate receiving e-mail, handwriting identifies you, much like a photo, to those you love. In years to come, someone will chance upon a letter you wrote and will be richer for it.

Recently, I came across letters I have saved from my son, from friends and from readers, many of which I treasure.

Some of the letters I found were from my father. His letters could move me, make me think, and make me proud. He rambles at times. (I think I inherited that characteristic from him.) But my father—even when he took a long time to say it—created a vivid picture of where he was, what he was doing, and especially, what he was feeling.

He wrote it. He seldom said it. He was not one to emote. Nor was he particularly outgoing in showing affection. He required it, and my mother, sister, and I obliged with lots of hugs and kisses. He, on the other hand, did not give strong embraces. But his face glowed when we showered him with love.

In his letters, he showed what made him tick. His love, caring, and intelligence are exposed in the familiar and legible (rare for a doctor) handwriting, which was between printing and calligraphy.

Until my mother died, there was no reason for him to write to me. I wasn't far away, and I would see my parents most weekends. When she died suddenly in January 1975, he was alone for the first time in his life. He wasn't well then (they were both hospitalized during Christmas in 1974) or in the four years he lived after that.

But he wrote to me almost every day. Then he wanted to say all that was on his mind. He allowed his heart to show, and to break, just by putting an exclamation point at the end of a sentence. I couldn't help but slide to the floor and read some of the letters again. It was as if he was talking to me and yes, at times, even hugging me.

There are days you need a hug.

I have him in my memory, which makes the letters come to life. But the reason for keeping them is to allow my son to know the grandfather he never really got to know. He died when my son was eight.

My father, not being well his last few years, was gruff. He was critical. He had forgotten that children make noise and run around a lot, so I think my son felt restricted with his grandfather. But his softer side, his concern for my son's future, and his love for him are in all these letters.

He wrote of the kindness of his apartment neighbors, his daily walks, the weather report, and appreciation for something as trivial as a thinly sliced Canadian bacon sandwich. He just penned what his life was on a daily basis. The simplest things sounded like poetry.

I had apologized for often typing my letters. He answered with, "Typed or handwritten, I'm thankful for all letters, just as long as they tell me you are well and happy."

We talked little about my divorce. But I knew he agonized. The way I knew was by reading his letters. He worried about his grandson's future.

"Don't let him play ball too often or for too long. The heat is dangerous." He worried. I, too, am a worrier.

When I would see him, he would say very little. When he wrote, he spoke volumes. Talking is good. Maybe it is even better than a letter, but when the talk is over, it's gone.

With a letter, you can have that conversation over and over again. Take pen in hand. Leave a legacy.

CONSTANT COMPANIONS

January 2003

A man and his dog. It's an age-old story, and yet I feel I must tell it one more time. The man lived in the family home, just up the street from where I live.

I never knew his name, but he died recently from injuries suffered in a fall on the ice in his driveway. He was out for his nightly walk with his dog, one of several outings on any given day. His name, I now know, was Robert Kohman.

I didn't know him except to say hello and maybe remark about the weather, and surely to talk about our dogs.

I first saw him in the late '60s, when I took my cocker spaniel to Mellon Park. Kohman was good-looking, but what really fascinated me was the way he treated his beautiful brown standard poodle, Fritz.

In those days, there were no leash laws and those of us who took our pets to Mellon Park for a run had a kind of club. Members knew the dogs' names but seldom knew the owner.

"How's Fritz?"

"How's Soot?"

We were identified by our pooches, and it was a friendly time in which I never witnessed a confrontation among the animals, from Dobermans and Great Danes to poodles or plain mutts.

I used to sit on a bench and watch Fritz and his owner.

The man would walk slowly to the end of the park, close to Fifth Avenue, leaving Fritz far behind on the grounds. He never looked back. And Fritz never budged, even if Soot would race up to him and rub noses.

A signal from his owner, way down the hill, would then send Fritz racing to obey. It was marvelous to watch such a well-trained animal, although I used to wonder whether this man allowed the dog on the furniture in his home.

At the park there was an atmosphere of play and toss, pant and drool, run and rest. Dogs and owners alike.

I would guess I observed this man for almost thirty-five years. After Fritz died, his loneliness was evident, but he soon had a golden retriever, another beautifully behaved dog named Randy. By that time, we lived on the same street, so I saw them often. And then, after a long life, that dog, too, was gone.

I wondered whether this man would get another dog, and sure enough one day I saw him with another golden retriever puppy straining at his leash as he walked him around the neighborhood. And that was Tyler.

Tyler had some early physical problems that concerned his owner, and he wasn't sure whether surgery would help. It could be genetic, he told me one day as we greeted each other. I could tell he was devastated at the thought of losing him.

But soon afterward, I saw the man walking Tyler, bandaged and wearing an impressive splint. Tyler survived, and he and my present cocker spaniel, also named Soot, have exchanged wet nose greetings for the past ten years.

I always thought Kohman walked with a military and disciplined bearing, so I wasn't surprised to learn he had a military background as a naval officer and a Merchant Marine.

I often saw him miles from his house several times in a given day. I was driving; he was walking his dog.

The past few years, it was painful to see this tall, straight gentleman walking more slowly as he began to have a definite curvature to his back. But he never gave up his daily walks, a garden trowel or plastic bag in one hand, through rain, snow, or heat.

Tyler had also slowed down from the frisky pup I first encountered. Together, they were a team, and they seemed to look out for each other.

It was Tyler's unusual and incessant barking which finally brought help hours after Kohman fell in his driveway. The dog never left his side.

Robert Kohman would have been eighty-one on December 26. He died December 24.

In the death notice, Tyler, who will now live with Kohman's niece, was the first name mentioned, surviving him as "his beloved golden retriever and constant companion." Some people might not understand that. It doesn't surprise me at all.

When designer Bill Blass died, it was noted, "By his side was his beloved Lab, Barnaby."

And so it goes. A man and his dog. I never tire of the story.

SPLENDOR IN THE GRASS

April 2003

Listening to news sources reporting the war in Iraq, I was, of course, struck by the horrors we witnessed in the photographs and read in the daily reports. But as graphic as so much of it was, I smiled at a soldier's reply to a TV reporter's question amid the frenzy of war.

The soldier was asked what he missed back home in North Carolina. The question didn't make me look up from my newspaper. The answer did.

"I miss the grass," he said.

Here was a Marine, not complaining, sitting atop a tank that was in sore need of a drive-through wash, just as he was in need of a hot bath, missing the sight of grass.

It was not a revelation exactly, but I was touched by the simplicity of his words. I just exhaled heavily.

He didn't say he missed a big car, Hooters, a gourmet dinner, or other tangible luxuries. He was sitting atop his temporary home, a tank, and he was wiping the inside of his helmet during a break in hostile fire. His face was dusty and smudged.

The answer must have surprised the embedded reporter as well.

Where do you go with grass? What's the next question? I didn't care. It was eloquent in its quiet way. He didn't try to be deep or to send a message to folks back home, or to be politically correct.

As we are into spring and grass is turning greener, we will soon complain about mowing and crabgrass and spots where grass won't grow.

This soldier was fighting for his right to sit and watch it grow, marvel at the work of nature, and yes, maybe complain about having to keep it cut week to week.

He has been looking at nothing but brown earth, sand and dirt and dust. And death and survival. Grass would look pretty darned good about now.

He did say, when pressed further, that he also missed "hearing his father talk" and "a pork chop sandwich would be nice."

He had me at grass.

The image, as his beige uniform blended with the desert and the tanks, was spectacular. I got up immediately and gazed at my small plot of grass, and the green lawns of my neighbors. I wished I could package it and send it to this Marine.

We take so much for granted. Even as I sit and watch the war news, I am comfy in my robe and slippers. I am undoubtedly munching on something good, or sipping a cool drink or morning coffee. I can see my forsythia from the window, and I will probably take in a movie or meet a friend for lunch. I doubt I will pay much attention to the grass.

We don't know what we will miss when deprived, but as this soldier revealed, it might be something simple.

You've heard the expression "the grass is always greener." We always think someone else has more, or better, and we are often wrong. We fail to appreciate what we have, what we look at every day.

I recently mentioned I didn't appreciate having a roof over my head until winds ripped under some shingles and water dripped into my sun porch. I awoke each morning never thinking about my nice warm house, until the furnace pilot went out when it was just 7 degrees outside and I began to shiver.

So, I look to more of the simple things each day, for which I am grateful. That includes any color sky, as long as no bombs are falling from it; a drink of water whenever I want.

A female soldier was asked about the best part of her day.

"Being able to wash my hair for the first time in weeks" was her reply. I've never thought washing my hair worth mentioning. If I couldn't, it would be a different story.

The men and women serving our country are the ones who can best tell us what we are fighting for and what really matters.

Another Marine has said he misses that time of day "when dinner is over, the dishes are done, and my wife dims the kitchen lights as the day winds down. I've put the kids to bed.

"I miss the warmth of the house at that time of day," he told a reporter.

No grandiose thoughts. It is so basically simple.

I doubt these men would have had the same answers if asked those questions before they were far from home and engaged in battles for survival.

As ugly as war is, it makes us take a good look at what is often taken for granted.

It's Easter Sunday. It's spring and a time for rebirth, even in the aftermath of war. The grass is growing and thanks to a young Marine, I feel I am seeing it for the first time.

A DISEASE WITH NO NAME

April 2006

As I watched the movie *Philadelphia* recently for the third or fourth time, it once again moved me—and reminded me. *Philadelphia* is, of course, about AIDS. I think it is the best work Tom Hanks has ever done. He deservedly won an Oscar.

The title could be any city. Take your pick. Yes, even Pittsburgh. No city is immune.

Longtime Companion was one of the first movies to put a face to AIDS in 1990. Hanks's film was made in 1993. His character was a son, a brother, an uncle, a lover, a friend, a human being.

The fashion world reeled when the illness began some twenty-five years ago. But Hanks's character in this film was a young lawyer, not a fashion designer.

I was working with people in the hard-hit fashion industry for almost thirty-five years, and some of those years, the late '70s through the '80s, were the years the strange and yet unnamed malady began to surface.

I remember the fear evolving as friend after friend came down with what would eventually, but not immediately, have a name— AIDS.

It was dreaded. It was mysterious. Everyone was scared. So many people were getting so sick. So many were dying.

My job as a fashion editor for the *Pittsburgh Press* took me to New York three or four times a year for seasonal fashion collections, beginning in 1960. For at least fifteen of those years, it was pure excitement, with very little serious thought beyond what would be trendy for the next season. I made many friends, gay as well as straight.

Then the fear began. We were afraid to use the same chip dip at a cocktail party if someone suspected of having this "virus" had preceded us. Don't hug, certainly don't kiss, even if on the cheek. It might even be best not to touch at all.

With each succeeding trip to Manhattan, in the '80s, we would hear about a few more in the designing world who were "suddenly ill" or who looked nothing like the person you had seen a short six months prior.

It would go beyond designers and artists. It would be publicists, executives, authors, and eventually not just men, but women we knew.

Often, when seeing a person with AIDS, we could only gasp. Many had developed Kaposi's sarcoma, all too evident on the skin. It was, we would soon learn, the Rock Hudson look.

I recall a well-liked publicist, who always sent his grandmother's fudge at Christmas, calling me one afternoon. His voice was raspy. He would explain he had a cold, but you knew. And you were right. We began, sadly, to know the telltale signs.

I leaned down often to hug someone in a wheelchair, someone still doing his collections or writing his columns, with the aid of assistants. But we were warned: Don't touch—as if the disease could be passed by such an innocent gesture of caring.

Last year, according to National AIDS Trust, more than three million people acquired HIV (human immune deficiency virus, which causes AIDS), which means an estimated forty million people are now living with HIV and AIDS. It is now a global emergency, claiming eight thousand lives every day.

By the time the rumor had spread that designer Perry Ellis had AIDS, there was at last a name for it.

Known for his boyish good looks and those giant strides he took around his runway after a show, a model on each arm, a beaming smile on his face, Ellis was gallant enough to be at his very last show. He looked nothing like himself. I had shared the elevator with him to his showroom, and I didn't recognize him.

During menswear press weeks those who were not afflicted, and a few who were—writers, publicists, manufacturers, and designers—began to have impromptu auctions, sometimes very silly things, like making bikinis out of whatever we could find in our hotel rooms or in our suitcases to raise money. We would cheer madly when someone pledged $100 or $500 for a bikini made out of a Bloomingdale's shopping bag or a beach towel, or even paper press releases.

Our friends were dying. We didn't know what else to do. We were helpless. But we hugged and cried and laughed and mourned together. And we thought it would go away.

There still is no cure, but HIV can be managed with a powerful cocktail of drugs to prevent the virus from exploding into AIDS. The multidrug therapy has allowed many infected patients to lead a somewhat normal life, but it doesn't work for everyone.

HIV has now spread beyond the fashion or the gay community—way beyond. We had no idea what we were witnessing all those years ago.

Most of us, all these years later, know someone who is ill or has died of what once had no name. It remains deadly. Sometimes I think we have forgotten. If you knew someone with AIDS, you can't forget.

MIRACLE ON THE MONITOR

April 2008

I have seen my granddaughter's face.

She is not due to arrive until later this month, but I have seen her—by sonogram. Isn't this an amazing world? As I await the birth of my first grandchild, this old granny has come face to face with advancements made over the past thirty-five-plus years since I had my own child at age forty-one.

Giving birth at that age doesn't seem like such an accomplishment now, but back then it was rare...and scary. My own father delivered hundreds of babies in his years of practicing medicine, and I remember he mentioned how "risky" a new patient's delivery would be. She was, after all, thirty years old.

That memory caused me to keep my condition unknown to him until I reached seven months. Doctors sometimes know too much. I was worried enough for everyone. No amnio, no sonogram. No tests for possible health problems for the baby. We just waited...and hoped. We knew very little. Now, it seems, the process, if not the act of birthing, has intensified, due to knowledge.

So everything changes. I traveled to the Fetal and Women's Center in Phoenix a few weeks ago to observe what I had never seen before. I lamented the fact I had forgotten to put film in my camera, and my son looked at me and said, "Mom, they have cameras here. That's why we are here."

He was smiling and shaking his head. He has always rolled his eyes at my camera-clicking passion. He didn't understand that what I wanted was to take pictures of him sitting behind his beloved Maggie, holding her hand, stroking her forehead as she lay on the table and they shared this moment. I would be discreet. I would not embarrass them. Maggie's mother, Frani, was with us. She has four grandchildren but had never seen this procedure. We were both awestruck.

As it happened, the moment was captured for all of us on the monitor on the wall as baby Gracie was or wasn't ready for her close-up. There she was, after twenty minutes or so of unidentified movement. The miracle on the monitor. The face of a sleeping child, content in her warm surroundings and, according to my son, "pouting."

We all let out a gasp when we saw her. Drew squeezed Maggie's hand and kissed her forehead. That's the picture I wanted. As it is, I hold it in my heart, not on film, as I am sure they do.

I am learning more every day about childbirth, even in my seventy-ninth year. My son and daughter-in-law know more than I do, even now, although the baby isn't due for several weeks. Books can inform you, but they never quite prepare you for the reality…the miracle.

I miscarried a first child very early. I never knew if it was to be a boy or a girl. In fact, until I lost that baby I had never been driven to be a mother. I didn't feel unfulfilled not having a child…until then. And fortunately, I was blessed with my son two years later.

My son never had a nursery, but then, neither did I. My grandchild will have more than either of us, materially. That's a good thing. I guess this will be one grandmother whose eyebrows will be constantly raised at the newness of it all, but who couldn't have more love for Gracie than I had thirty-seven years ago when I first held my son and became a mom…for real. That's the miracle.

How did our babies make it without all of these gadgets? It makes one wonder how we made it to the twenty-first century. Or lived to tell about it. Thank goodness I did. I am looking at a picture of Grace Elizabeth, sleeping in her mother's womb, as I write. Can you believe that?

AMAZING GRACE

May 2008

You won't faint, will you?"

That was the question I was asked when I learned I could watch the arrival of Grace Elizabeth Marie Cloud, my new granddaughter. I felt sure I wouldn't. And, I didn't. However, my mouth was agape through the whole process. Of that I can assure you.

She was born at 5:36 p.m. April 30 in Scottsdale Healthcare Hospital in Arizona. She weighed an ounce short of 9 pounds and was 22 inches long.

The most common answer to most of my questions, then and now, is, "Oh, they don't do that anymore." It has been a few years since I have paid attention to a newborn.

No sterile white delivery room and no doctors and nurses in white gowns and caps and masks over their faces. I've seen too many TV hospital shows. I thought of my father, who delivered hundreds of babies in his fifty-year career as a physician, from the 1920s to the '70s. If my eyes were popping, his would have been even more so.

It has all changed. There is no sterile white. There are no swinging doors as the gurney carrying the pregnant woman swings open into the "delivery room" with bright spotlights hanging overhead and, as imagined, a woman wailing in pain. Not at this birth. It was unusually quiet and serene, although seventeen hours had passed since my daughter-in-law, Maggie, entered the hospital.

I had never seen a baby born, except my own thirty-seven years ago, and that was definitely from another angle.

Maggie was magnificent. To have my son, Drew, holding her hand and stroking her brow during the push counts made me so proud. Her mother, Frani, and sister, Christy, were also in the room and, would you believe, the television was on! The doctor, who had just delivered another baby down the hall and was awaiting a third delivery on the same floor, wandered in and out as Maggie's contractions got closer. When he finally declared, "She's complete," Maggie started pushing. He even did some paperwork at a nearby table while we waited.

Unlike Dr. Welby, Dr. Kildare, and all those other TV doctors I have identified with through the years (and certainly not Dr. McDreamy or Dr. McSteamy who heat up today's TV screens), this doctor was cool, collected, and uncomplicated.

Even as Drew cut the umbilical cord, he was calm…but complications came within fifteen minutes as what they labeled a "traumatic birth" had somehow taken its toll on Grace and she was not responding as they had wished after being toweled and suctioned, swaddled and capped and held by her adoring parents and grandparents.

After much jubilation and photo snapping, attending aides' brows were furrowed, and a call went out to doctors in the babies' special care unit. They wanted to monitor Grace overnight. She appeared lethargic and was not interested in taking a bottle.

The room suddenly grew silent when the baby's bassinet was wheeled back into the room, minus Grace, after she was taken to special care.

The next day we learned she had pneumonia, which, surprising as it was, was better than not knowing what was wrong. Antibiotics kicked in and even with feeding tubes and oxygen she appeared healthy but was simply worn out by her birth experience. During the next seven days in the special care unit we could still hold her, rock her, and marvel at her as she was weaned from the oxygen as well as the feeding tube in her nose and she began to take her nourishment by bottle every three hours.

Grace is now healthy and at home, getting used to her nursery, her Boppy, her headbands with perky bows and flowers, soft music by her crib, tummy-time, cooing, and a bit of sniffing and curiosity from Lambert, her canine protector who was the first baby in the house a little more than a year ago.

Yes, much has changed in medicine, but the smell of a new baby, the marvel of ten fingers and ten toes, the stretching of tiny legs and arms, the murmurs while sleeping, and the dreams for her future…they're priceless.

ABOUT THE AUTHOR

Born in Uniontown, Pennsylvania, the third daughter of the late Dr. Milton Harlan and Elizabeth Miller Cloud (their first daughter, Ethelyn, died shortly after birth—and her older sister, Betty Joyce, died in June 1998, at age seventy), Barbara Cloud graduated from Uniontown Senior High School and Westminster College, New Wilmington, Pennsylvania, where she majored in speech and drama.

A former president of the Women's Press Club, she received many honors during her career as a journalist: Pennsylvania Newspapers Publishers Association Best Local Column, 1961; 1961-62 Golden Quills; Alumni Achievement Award from Westminster College, 1968; the FRANY (Fashion Reporters Award New York), 1970; Western Pennsylvania Chapter of the National Society of Interior Designers first recognition award for daily influence upon lives of readers in the tri-state area, 1971; listed in *Who's Who in American Colleges and Universities*; Allegheny County Medical Society Association Award for Better Living in Pittsburgh, 1986; Hadassah's Special Gratitude Award for incisive commentary, 1987; Men's Fashion Association Aldo award for a single feature, and later, MFA's Lifetime Achievement Golden Aldo, 1991.

She resides in the Squirrel Hill section of Pittsburgh with her rescued cocker spaniel, Nash. Her hobby is photography and her home is filled with photos of Pittsburgh, the beach, and of course, her first grandchild.

WA